An Education

John Walshe was born in Galway and is a past pupil of St Joseph's College, Galway, and a graduate of both NUIG and UCC. Before becoming special adviser to the Minister for Education and Skills, Ruairi Quinn, in 2011, he had spent four decades writing about education issues, mostly with the *Irish Independent* but also for two years with the *Irish Times*. He is a three-times winner of national media awards and has been a consultant to the OECD on a number of education reports. He has three children, Conor, Maria and Bryan. A widower, he lives in Bray, County Wicklow.

An Education

*How an outsider became an
insider – and learned what really
goes on in Irish government*

JOHN WALSHE

PENGUIN
IRELAND

PENGUIN IRELAND

Published by the Penguin Group
Penguin Ireland, 25 St Stephen's Green, Dublin 2, Ireland
(a division of Penguin Books Ltd)
Penguin Books Ltd, 80 Strand, London WC2R 0RL, England
Penguin Group (USA) Inc., 375 Hudson Street, New York, New York 10014, USA
Penguin Group (Australia), 707 Collins Street, Melbourne, Victoria 3008, Australia
(a division of Pearson Australia Group Pty Ltd)
Penguin Group (Canada), 90 Eglinton Avenue East, Suite 700, Toronto, Ontario, Canada M4P 2Y3
(a division of Pearson Penguin Canada Inc.)
Penguin Books India Pvt Ltd, 11 Community Centre, Panchsheel Park, New Delhi – 110 017, India
Penguin Group (NZ), 67 Apollo Drive, Rosedale, Auckland 0632, New Zealand
(a division of Pearson New Zealand Ltd)
Penguin Books (South Africa) (Pty) Ltd, Block D, Rosebank Office Park,
181 Jan Smuts Avenue, Parktown North, Gauteng 2193, South Africa

Penguin Books Ltd, Registered Offices: 80 Strand, London WC2R 0RL, England

www.penguin.com

First published 2014
001

Copyright © John Walshe, 2014

The moral right of the author has been asserted

Set in 13.5/16 pt Garamond MT Std
Typeset by Jouve (UK), Milton Keynes
Printed in Great Britain by Clays Ltd, St Ives plc

A CIP catalogue record for this book is available from the British Library

ISBN: 978–1–844–88360–8

www.greenpenguin.co.uk

In memory of
my parents, Betty and Captain Jack,
the best educators I ever had

Author's note

In recalling, checking and writing the material that follows I have drawn both from the diary I kept during my time as a special adviser and also from the diary of Ruairi Quinn. He recorded his thoughts daily until late 2012 and for this book he very kindly allowed me access to, and permission to use, material relating to political and governmental business.

Contents

CONTENTS

Prologue

On 2 July 2014, RTÉ's *Morning Ireland* set off alarm bells in half a dozen households scattered across the Greater Dublin Area. Among the items coming up, announced Audrey Carville, would be Minister Pat Rabbitte 'on marriage equality, broadband and possible retirement'.

'Oh feck, he's going to gazump us,' was my immediate response. I knew it was exactly what my boss, Minister for Education and Skills Ruairi Quinn, and other members of his team would be thinking. We had made meticulous plans in secret to announce his retirement from the Cabinet later that day and now it looked like Rabbitte was going to get there first. Sure enough, the texts started straightaway.

But Rabbitte didn't. Instead, when interviewer Cathal Mac Coille asked him if it was time to go, he attacked the ageist attitude implicit in the question. He made it clear he wanted to stay in the Cabinet even after Eamon Gilmore, his lifelong friend from their days in student politics, was replaced as party leader two days later.

Greatly relieved by Rabbitte's characteristic truculence, I hopped on the DART for what was to be a momentous day, one of many since I'd taken on the exciting, at times exhausting, job as special adviser to Ruairi Quinn in April 2011. When I arrived in the department he was in his first floor office – early as usual – and was drinking the first or second of his countless cups of coffee. He was quite calm about the day ahead.

We had a brief chat about the planned choreography of the announcement. We shook hands and I thanked him for giving me the opportunity to work as his special adviser, and wished him luck, before repairing to my office upstairs. Ruairi's time, and mine, in the magnificent Tyrone House was drawing to a close, reminding me of what the previous Labour education minister Niamh Bhreathnach had said to me in Leinster House more than three years earlier: 'Ruairi and you should enjoy it – it will be over before you think.'

The tempo began to pick up quickly that morning with further tweaking of Ruairi's speech, which Neil Ward – who was to become my successor and was a political-party animal, unlike me – had drafted. After further consultations with press officer Deirdre Grant, it was off to his final gig in IBEC House in Lower Leeson Street. The organizers had called to ask if he could come early. They wanted to take pictures of the minister with representatives of the business and employers' organization IBEC and the Institutes of Technology Ireland, which was launching a new R&D innovation strategy. I said yes, and repeated that we had to leave no later than 10.45.

Once there, I made it clear that even if somebody was in full flow, we were leaving the event at the appointed time. I went so far as to show them the door beside the podium from which we would exit. The four speakers got the message and fairly rattled through the speeches. With minutes to spare, I hustled Ruairi out, past the inevitable 'A quick word, Minister' requests, told him there were two journalists in the foyer who wanted to ask about issues of the day, whom he agreed to talk to, and then we were back safely in the car. I rang Deirdre to update her and she then ordered that the media invitations for a noon announcement on the plinth at Leinster House be released at exactly eleven o'clock.

The plinth has acquired a special symbolism in Irish politics. It's the slightly raised area in front of Leinster House from where the then freshly elected TD Fine Gael's Mary Mitchell O'Connor famously tried to drive (leading to a hefty repair bill from her mechanic). But it's best known as a venue for major announcements made by politicians who are usually surrounded by their colleagues and supporters. We were determined that the announcement would be made by Ruairi alone, with no 'doughnut' of advisers or supporters around him.

The phones were hopping as soon as we were back on the marbled Ministerial Corridor in Leinster House. Deirdre was fielding the calls and politely told all the hacks nothing, either on or off the record – no detail before the noon announcement. Getting nowhere with Deirdre, they tried ringing Neil and me. The only call I answered was from my good friend Katherine Donnelly of the *Irish Independent*, but I told her that I couldn't help her. I didn't respond to anybody else, including RTÉ's Sean O'Rourke. I didn't reply to his text 'Is he going?' so Sean tried ringing me when he was off air during an ad break. Couldn't blame him – it would have been a scoop to have confirmation before the noon announcement.

The tension was rising on the corridor, as it was 11.25 and Ruairi still had not told the Taoiseach or Tánaiste of his decision. The Tánaiste was ensconced with Minister Brendan Howlin in Eamon's office. So Ruairi and Neil sat down with Mark Garrett, the Tánaiste's chief of staff, to tell him what was happening and say that Eamon had to talk to Ruairi urgently. Eamon quickly finished his meeting with Howlin, went into Ruairi's office and closed the door.

Ruairi's team, including me, waited in his private secretary's office, which is a few yards directly across the corridor. That office was shared by Minister Phil Hogan's private secretary. Hogan was usually in and out regularly but, fortunately, he wasn't around that morning. He would have immediately known something was up, and it wouldn't have taken him long to winkle it out of one of us. Up close and personal, Hogan can be very persuasive. Minister Brendan Howlin came into the unusually crowded office and must have wondered what the hell we were all doing there in our best bib and tucker – the men were in their smart suits and the women had obviously been to the hairdresser's – but he didn't ask. Neither did any of the other ministers or advisers passing by or dropping in for a bit of gossip.

After a few minutes Eamon came out and walked straight over to me. I've known Gilmore since his time as a student leader. 'Johnny, Ruairi was a great reforming minister,' he said, and we chatted for a bit.

Meanwhile, Ruairi managed to get the Taoiseach on the phone and told him of his decision. The clock was ticking and Joan Burton was in her office down the corridor. Though not yet elected, she was clearly going to be the next Labour Party leader, and she needed to be told too. Her advisers Ed Brophy and Karen O'Connell had been aware that something was up from earlier that morning and had asked Neil for an explanation. He rebuffed them initially, as we all had the journalists. But now that both the Taoiseach and Tánaiste were in the loop, the position changed. He pulled them out of a meeting they were attending with Joan and her officials. She realized something significant was happening and came with them. Neil briefed all three in agriculture minister Simon Coveney's empty office across the corridor. Her

4

immediate response was gratitude – she felt Ruairi's decision was incredibly generous, and one that would save her an awkward situation during the impending reshuffle. She rushed down to Ruairi's office in double-quick time to thank him herself.

Ruairi's door was closed again. As the minutes ticked by, a member of Joan's staff was panicking outside the door because she was due in the Seanad at exactly 11.45 and, the staffer said, 'She has to get her make-up done.' With a minute to spare, we had to barge in and get her out.

Though nobody gave Alex White, Joan's opponent in the leadership race, any chance of winning the contest, as a courtesy, Ruairi was keen to inform him of his decision. Unfortunately, Alex wasn't in the building. We managed to brief his political adviser on what was about to play out so that Alex would not be blindsided by the events of the day.

We left Ruairi alone for a few moments to compose himself, and then we all walked together down the Ministerial Corridor and over the bridge that brings you to the back of the Dáil Chamber for the last time. The Taoiseach was just about to enter the chamber; I was walking beside Ruairi, so he came over to shake hands with the two of us, wishing us well. We all proceeded along the passageway at the side of the chamber and down the stairs. Ruairi kept his thoughts to himself as we walked towards the foyer. Then it was out the door to a battery of cameras and waiting journalists. We all moved to the side while six-times minister Ruairi Quinn announced that he was stepping down from politics at the next election and would not seek to serve in government after the change of Labour leadership.

TV 3's Ursula Halligan was first, with the question 'Was it prompted by petulance?' Ursula doesn't always ask the obvious, and many's the politician who fell into the trap of giving her daft or revealing answers. But in Deirdre's dry run of what Ruairi would be asked, she had primed him to expect the inevitable 'Did you jump before you were pushed?', so he had a ready response. In my experience, petulance was not one of his traits. Other questions flowed thick and fast, mostly generous and open-ended, and when finally asked what was his finest achievement, Ruairi quipped, 'How long do you have?'

Having made his announcement, it was time for photographs with party colleagues and then with his team, after which he returned to his office to deal with a flurry of phone calls. As arranged, Deirdre told the media there would be no more interviews. Also as arranged, we headed out an hour later for a long liquid and emotional lunch and finally repaired to Toner's bar in Baggot Street.

Later, much later, I got a lift to the DART. I took my seat and promptly fell asleep, waking up in Greystones, past my stop in Bray.

'Where did it all go so quickly?' I asked myself.

1. An offer I couldn't refuse

The phone call from Ruairi Quinn came out of the blue. He was only a couple of weeks in the job as Minister for Education and Skills and was beginning to make waves. What story was he going to give me? I naturally wondered when I agreed to meet him late that afternoon in Buswells, the great stomping ground for politicians, those who orbit them and the media. As I was mounting the steps of the hotel, a fleeting thought crossed my mind that maybe this was about more than giving me some story, but I dismissed it.

The hotel was not particularly busy and Ruairi was in a quiet area of the lounge, having coffee. After the initial hellos, he came straight to the point: 'I want you to be my special adviser, the salary is €80,000 and I'd like you to start immediately.' I was flummoxed and flattered at the same time.

Why me? I thought when I got over the surprise. I was not a member of the Labour Party (or, indeed, any political party). His proposition was simple. In opposition, he had been Labour's education spokesperson, so he knew the broad contours of the system but needed somebody to fill in the details. He also needed somebody to tell him who was who. Many of the education partners are very good at their jobs, but some don't always see the dots joining up into the bigger picture. Their answer to every problem is invariably to pitch for more 'resources' – the euphemism for taxpayers' money. One of the tasks I would have as a special adviser would be to tell him the best people to get things done, and the people who would not automatically push out the begging bowl in the middle of the biggest financial crisis the country had ever faced.

I had obviously come across Ruairi many times in my career as education editor with the *Irish Independent*, and not just since he had become opposition spokesperson three years earlier. He had impressed me in the eighties when he was in the Department of Labour and was trying to reorganize various services and agencies into what became FÁS. I had a huge interest in the whole area of youth employment, training and apprenticeships at the time and wrote often about what he was trying to achieve. We were of the same vintage – children of the post-Second World War decade who had been in college in the sixties – and shared the same views on the need to reform the education and training systems, as we discovered, sitting beside each other at dinners during various educational conferences.

He captured my surprise in his diary the next morning, where he noted that I was 'completely bowled over by my request to him to become my senior adviser. I am to meet him today to discuss a few matters. I feel he will take it, and I certainly hope so. We then have to run with the agenda and make things happen.'

Since it was something I had always wanted – to be on the inside, as opposed to observing and writing from the outside – I didn't need much convincing to say yes. We met again the next morning in the Gresham Hotel to discuss his offer in more detail. He wanted to announce my appointment in the department immediately, but I said to let me sort out the *Indo* first, in terms of notice and pension arrangements. We discussed briefly his priorities, especially Junior Cert reform and the issues of pluralism and patronage. As we concluded our conversation, we walked together up Marlborough Street – he back to his office in the Department of Education and Skills (DES) and me back to my desk around the corner in Independent House on Talbot Street.

'And, John, we'll have fun!' he called after me as I left him at the gates of the department. It was strange, but not sad, to be thinking about saying farewell to newspapers after more than forty years as an education journalist. This is as good as it gets, I thought to myself.

Education was Ruairí Quinn's dream Cabinet job. But he had been far from certain he would get it. In the late February 2011 general election, Labour and Fine Gael were returned to power with a thumping big majority, the best ever results for either party. Nine days later, on 6 March, Labour delegates to a special conference voted overwhelmingly to enter into a coalition with Fine Gael. Simultaneously, Fine Gael's seventy-six TDs were meeting in the Shelbourne Hotel to be briefed on the new Programme for Government. Afterwards, the two party leaders – Enda Kenny and Eamon Gilmore – met for a photo-call in Herbert Park to mark the formation of the coalition. Now the great guessing game was underway: who would and who would not make the ministerial cut?

'Am I being passed over, have I made the wrong decision to stay on, will I be in the Cabinet? Should I ask, how do you ask and what the hell anyway,' Ruairí wrote in his diary on the morning of Tuesday, 8 March – the day before Enda Kenny was sworn in as Taoiseach and the identity of the new ministers would be revealed. Then he did the secular equivalent of counting his blessings by noting how well his beloved family was.

The following morning, he wrote: 'The feelings have not

changed and the newspapers do not give me much comfort. I will take whatever comes and master it as well as I can. Dignity and decorum are the watchwords in defeat, if that is what it is going to be for me. I received much support from the people on the street when I walked in this morning. That in itself is positive, and Senator Fidelma Healy Eames [the Fine Gael senator who had a special interest in education] rang to wish me well, hoping that I would get the job of education, which is what I would love to get. But life will go on, no matter what.'

Later, he wrote that he 'was unable to concentrate at all during the morning and went out for a walk into the National Gallery and then back. The house filled up for the Taoiseach's vote (to elect the new Taoiseach). Then a snatched lunch in the Members' Bar. And an excruciating wait until Mark Garrett called me over the bridge to be taken down the corridor to meet Eamon. It is education, he said, and spoke briefly about a few things. Then the rush to the bus to the Aras. Willie Penrose [Minister of State for Housing and Planning] and Máire Whelan [Attorney General] are the big story.' His own private diary clearly contradicts an *Irish Times* report at the time that he had thrown a wobbly and demanded a seat in the Cabinet, which, it claimed, he achieved at the expense of his front-bench colleague Róisín Shortall.

He barely had his feet under the desk in Marlborough Street when he surprised officials by saying he would address the annual conference of the Catholic Primary School Management Association two days later. The officials in the department believed that he should read his way into his new portfolio and get a series of briefings on the major issues first. But he jumped at the chance to set out his stall as soon as possible – as he said in his opening remarks to the conference: 'Today's conference is my first public engagement as Minister, and I hope my presence here signals my intention to hit the ground running in addressing some of the many pressing issues that need to be tackled in the education system and in the primary sector in particular.'

He then confirmed a Programme for Government commitment to set up a Forum on Pluralism and Patronage. This was taken from the Labour pre-election manifesto, the education section of which had been largely written by his eager adviser, Ian O'Mara. Ian's father, Ciaran, had been Ruairi's special adviser when he was Minister for Finance, and Ian worked with Ruairi in the local Labour branch in Sandymount.

Ruairi's presence at the conference and his announcement of the forum indicated his determination to get things moving as quickly as possible. He assembled the rest of his team over the next couple of weeks. Ministers are usually allowed two special advisers, and some other staff who are officially categorized as personal or parliamentary assistants. They generally call themselves something else. Ian came with him into the department with the title Political Adviser. Neil Ward, a former youth officer and a rising star in the party's backrooms, was the Political Liaison, and Denise Rogers, Ruairi's hard-working office organizer throughout his political life, was an automatic choice for the team and had the title Secretary. (Denise is credited with the inspired choice of Mary Robinson as Labour's candidate for the presidency in 1990. 'She is someone who would make a difference,' she said to Ruairi early that year. Fergus Finlay heard the remark, passed it on to Dick Spring and John Rogers SC, who approached Robinson in February.)

That left him with the two special-adviser roles to fill – one would perform the function of press officer and the other would be his programme manager – and so he picked up the phone to me.

When Sean Flynn of the *Irish Times* joined Professor Alan Ahearne and myself at an NUI dinner in Galway sometime later, he quipped, 'Ah, the man who destroyed the economy talking to the man who is about to destroy the education system.' Ahearne had been Brian Lenihan's special adviser in the Department of Finance at the height of Ireland's banking crisis. The light-hearted comment echoed throughout the media and the public's sometimes suspicious view of the role of special advisers. It is an understandable viewpoint, since the role is ill-defined.

Ministerial advisers have been around since the 1973–7 coalition, and they still are very much a mixed bag. There are some serious academic studies on the role of the adviser in Ireland, notably by TCD's Eunan O'Halpin and by University of Limerick researcher Bernadette Connaughton, whose 2010 paper in *Irish Political Studies* 'Glorified Gofers, Policy Experts or Good Generalists: A Classification of the Roles of the Irish Ministerial Adviser' carried an interesting survey of advisers in service from 2000 to 2007. They did not conform to any particular type. They were picked by ministers for very different reasons. Some wanted glorified constituency gofers, some wanted policy specialists, some wanted experts, but most wanted good generalists to cover as many bases as possible.

All of those I dealt with came to the job with a different set of skills and background, and they all see the task in slightly different ways – working on policies, minding the minister's back, picking up political banana skins before the minister walks on them, being the minister's eyes and ears and, sometimes, voice, when he or she is not available, turning a blind eye occasionally, acting as a filter, liaising with department officials and others to further the minister's agenda, writing or checking speeches and Dáil and Seanad contributions, reading a tsunami of daily emails and reports, keeping an eye on the Cabinet agenda, attending the Senior Officials Group (SOG) and countless other meetings. And so on.

My view of what kind of adviser I was going to be was shaped by the two conversations I had with Ruairí about his expectations. My main role, as I saw it, was to help and shape his agenda and use my educational contacts to achieve that goal. But I was well aware that tapping contacts for news stories is very different from getting them to cooperate with change. I was also aware that it was a huge leap from covering education to being at the very heart of policy discussion and formation.

There is no manual for the job of ministerial adviser, but there was no shortage of suggestions either from the old hands or from the apparatchiks in the party whom the public never see. 'Use Post-it notes, don't put it in an email if it's sensitive, because it can be FOIed' (i.e. sought out by a member of the media or the public under the Freedom of Information Act), was the wise advice from one who knew the pitfalls for the unwary. A senior Labour aide instructed the new bunch of advisers simply not to 'get captured by your department', and a third said that 'Advisers shouldn't just have a low profile, they should have no profile.' The Fine Gael-appointed government press secretary Feargal Purcell, who was a military man much given to using unusual metaphors, told us that 'We have to stop our ministers driving over their own landmines.' It took me some time to realize the wisdom behind the words of one former Fianna Fáil adviser: 'Don't tell fellow advisers too much, as they will try to make mischief.' But the best advice was 'keep a diary', which I did.

The final member of the team, Ruairi's second special adviser, was Deirdre Grant, who joined us a few weeks later. Ministers can appoint their own press officers, who are either career civil servants or are brought in from outside. Deirdre had been a news reporter with TV3 news from its inception and was later political correspondent with INN. She would coordinate the work of the relatively small press office in the department and was one of the best PR people I ever came across.

Ironically, it was April Fool's Day when I officially went on secondment from Independent Newspapers, and the following Monday – 4 April 2011 – I said hello to my new job as an unestablished civil servant. The duration of my unexpected encore career was dependent on Ruairi. He made it clear to all of us that our jobs would last as long as he was in ministerial office. That, of course, would not stop anybody leaving earlier if they wished.

Before starting, I had a long chat with the secretary general of the department, Brigid McManus. She was full of enthusiasm for change after a succession of relatively unadventurous ministers. But she was also clear that there were boundary lines between her statutory duties and my role – as yet undefined – with department officials.

I had known many of the other officials before I arrived and now made it my business to spend at least an hour with each of the ten assistant secretaries to find out their areas of responsibility. They were all very courteous and helpful. Pat

Burke, who had the tricky job of handling industrial relations with the unions, was the quintessential civil servant and
told me I would know I was accepted when people in the
department started phoning me for advice. They did come
round to it. One official suggested that I should seek to
breach the salary cap set down by the government, as special
advisers in other departments were clearly doing. I was told I
could argue that, because of my experience involved in writing four education reports for the Paris-based international
think tank the Organization for Economic Cooperation
and Development (OECD), in addition to writing for the
newspapers, I should get more money. But I guessed, rightly
as it turned out, that some of my new colleagues would be
pilloried in the media for doing just that, so I said no, keep
me on the principal officers' scale. When other ministers
were subsequently trying to defend their special advisers'
level of pay, Ruairi was able to say his were all within the pay
guidelines.

I had a choice of offices on the top floor of Tyrone House,
and the one I opted for was certainly the biggest I had ever
had, with a six-seater conference table and, in no time at all, a
constantly untidy desk. Visitors for meetings often admired
the old fireplace – I used to joke that it wasn't in use any
more, as you couldn't get good staff nowadays to light a
decent fire. Directly opposite me was the press office, busy at
times, and a great place for tea and cakes for birthday parties.
On the floor below me were the fine offices of the minister
and secretary general of the department. They faced out on
to Marlborough Street, at the front of the imposing Georgian building that was originally the Dublin townhouse for
Marcus Beresford, Earl of Tyrone. Each had their own office
staff, who were kept pretty busy, frantically so at times, except

in the dead month of August. Next door to Ruairi's office were Neil, Ian and Denise, but sometime later Neil moved upstairs to yet another empty office.

The first few weeks were a blur – new names, new faces, a mountain of material to read, preparations to make for the forthcoming teachers' conferences, and so on. And that was on top of frequent trips over to Government Buildings for yet more meetings. Every Monday, the Fine Gael and Labour special advisers met to discuss the items coming up at the next day's Cabinet meeting. There was a sense of excitement at the first few meetings, of believing that one was in a powerful position at the right time and could make a contribution to important decisions. After a while, I could see that they weren't all they were cracked up to be. Separately, the Labour advisers started meeting on Wednesdays, not just the special advisers but press officers and other staffers. These were much less serious and formal than the Monday meetings and helped outsiders such as myself bond more closely with the party's thinking and strategies.

After the first few weeks, I was beginning to see the trees from the wood and realized there was so much going on I would have to focus on priorities. It was too easy to get sucked into detail and I had to learn to pull back and let others do some of the hard work. Besides, I didn't have time, as I was being constantly pulled into meetings with Ruairi and various officials. We agreed among ourselves on the team that one of us would always be with Ruairi when he met a deputation to note what was being said and provide back-up if necessary. Ruairi's diary secretary, Deirdre Brabazon, took to asking me for advice on which of the myriad requests for meetings or to speak at conferences I would recommend for his consideration.

In the first few weeks in the job I also got a couple of invitations to speak at conferences. I had doubts about the wisdom of doing it, in case anything I said was taken down and used as evidence of Ruairi's thinking. I asked him for his opinion. He didn't say yes and didn't say no, just remarked, 'You wouldn't want to be developing a public personality of your own now, would you?' In a previous coalition, strong personalities such as Dick Spring's special adviser Fergus Finlay had become too public and given rise to disquiet about powerful unelected advisers. We did operate as a team, but there was never any doubt that Ruairi was the boss. He wasn't dogmatic about it, just a natural leader.

2. Hitting the ground running

After six months in office, Ruairi was reflecting on how he was enjoying being back in government: 'I know what I am doing and more importantly why I am doing it. I understand the briefs and the agenda and indeed have written much of it. This is my fifth full Cabinet job and I intend to make the reforms and changes that the country needs. It is going to be my last term in executive Cabinet office. That I know, and I intend to make a real mark of progressive and radical change.' A month later, he wrote, 'I had a most satisfactory breakfast meeting with Enda Kenny. He, like me, is loving the job!' Having been around the Ministerial Corridor on four previous occasions, and once as a Minister of State, he knew the ropes and relished being back in the Cabinet for the last time.

He wasn't a 'three day week' rural minister who drove up from the country on Monday and home on Thursday evening to nurse the constituency. He didn't neglect his constituency, but Ruairi effectively handed over 'ownership' of Dublin Bay South to fellow TD Kevin Humphreys and his councillors, as he didn't expect to stand again in the next general election, due in 2016, which would coincide with his seventieth birthday. This meant he could spend an unusually large number of hours a week on task in the department.

Marlborough Street was to be our main working base, but a lot of time was also spent in Government Buildings. As a minister and TD, Ruairi naturally had to spend much time

there on Oireachtas business, Cabinet meetings and committee meetings, delegations, and so on.

His office was beside Eamon Gilmore's. It was originally
to have been Pat Rabbitte's, and Ruairi's designated office
was on another corridor nearby, with other ministers. The
share-out of offices wasn't to do with any natural pecking
order, just space limitations. But Ruairi wanted to be near the
Tánaiste, and he moved in his boxes and books before Rabbitte got a chance.

It was not a huge office: it just had a desk, a television and a
small conference table, where, over the coming forty months,
Ruairi would hold innumerable meetings with us, his officials,
political colleagues, official delegations and other visitors. The
books on his window ledge were always interesting – history,
education and politics mainly, never a novel: Ruairi didn't do
novels.

But he saw his main mission as driving education reforms.
He was often the first into the department in the morning,
and attended to some educational business before heading
off to Leinster House for Cabinet meetings, or other business. Ruairi usually went by car, to save time.

Special advisers also have to go to Government Buildings
regularly. Our office in Marlborough Street was one of the
furthest away. At a brisk walk, it was almost fifteen minutes
to Leinster House in Kildare Street. That's around half an
hour there and back, and invariably I bumped into someone
I knew who would delay me further, usually when I was busy
and didn't have time for a chat. Apart from walking, my
options were to cadge a lift from the minister's driver, if he
was available, get the bus or taxi in an emergency, or join the
Dublin Bike Scheme. I opted for the last, and often cycled to

and from Leinster House with confidential documents stuffed into my inside pocket.

Ruairi's long hours gave him time to forge a massive reform agenda, affecting primary, secondary and further education and training, and higher education. At the outset, he decided to avoid the Irish language as a battle too far, as Enda Kenny had discovered when he raised the issue in the run-up to the general election and alienated many in the still-powerful language lobby. Leaving Certificate students have to study Irish – unless they can call on an exemption, usually for health-related reasons or because of diagnosed learning difficulties or they were born overseas – but they don't have to sit it in the exam. Kenny wanted to retain Irish as compulsory for Junior Certificate students but only as an option at Leaving Certificate level. Ruairi wisely decided not to pursue it; it would have sapped time and energy he wanted to expend elsewhere.

To get his reform agenda through, he needed the support of the department, and some officials were upset by harsh comments about them he made when he was in opposition. They remembered in particular his comments in June 2009, when he had said that there was a continuing culture of deferment and obedience to the Catholic Church in the department. He complained that he had been trying for months to get information about the nature, location and names of the schools in the ownership of religious orders or Roman Catholic bishops. However, the department had refused to provide such information in replies to Dáil questions. 'Either officials in the department are members of secret societies, such as the Knights of St Columbanus and Opus Dei, and have taken it upon themselves to protect the interests of these clerical orders . . . or, alternatively, the minister [Fianna Fáil's Batt O'Keeffe] is politically incompetent and incapable of managing the department.'

He made a direct appeal for support when he addressed his first Min-MAC – a ministerial meeting with the department's Management Advisory Committee. He told Brigid McManus and ten assistant secretary generals that his comments were on the Dáil record, and he hoped that the department's staff would prove them wrong.

Brigid promised support, and was as good as her word. In the months that followed, it was obvious that any stereotypes about the department – including Ruairi's – were well out of date and things had moved on considerably from the day when there was said to be a side stairs in the department dubbed *staighre na n-easpag* which brought members of the Catholic hierarchy directly up to the minister's floor. (Having said that, there were occasional glimpses of what it might have been like in the old days. Assistant secretary general Martin Hanevy had a funny story about waiting to sign off on the redeployment of a couple of primary-school teachers with the patron of a school, the local bishop, only to be told the bishop was on retreat and couldn't be disturbed. He had to wait a few days until his lordship was available.)

The Archbishop of Dublin, Diarmuid Martin, was one of the few members of the Catholic hierarchy to come into the department over the forty months of Ruairi's term of office. Indeed, I met more Church of Ireland clergymen than Catholic bishops during my time there. As for the Irish language, I heard little Irish spoken and saw only one *fáinne*.

Brigid McManus was one of the brightest people I ever met. In journalism, you are told there are always two sides to a story, but Brigid could see three, four or five of them before she gave her considered and nuanced response. This was an intellectual strength but could sometimes lead to analysis paralysis, which delayed decisions and submissions to the minister. Over the coming months and years, we would get to know the strengths and weaknesses of the individual MAC members. They were hard-working, intelligent, decent people to work with. They generally had a great facility with words and their memos could enlighten or obscure or gloss over difficulties with a few deft phrases.

The MAC was where it was at, as far as the department was concerned. It was the venue for thrashing out important issues, and it was where I wanted to be in attendance every week. No such luck. Special advisers attend MAC meetings in some but not all other departments, and Labour was encouraging its advisers to insist on entry to them all so that we would know what was happening. But Brigid made it clear to me that if I pushed it too much, then the DES management would simply create a new forum where issues could be freely debated without a special adviser whose presence would only change the dynamic and inhibit discussion. Nothing personal, just department business.

Gradually, as the officials got to know the temporary staff, as Ruairi dubbed himself and his team, working relations became very good. The civil service can be a bit like a chameleon, adapting to its natural surroundings. If ministers want a relatively untroubled time, particularly in the run-up to a general election, that's fine. But if there is a minister who creates what Martin Hanevy and Pat Burke called 'noise in the system', it will also handle it. In the DES, the officials responded well to a challenging minister who wanted to drive change. If anything, Ruairi was fortunate in his timing, despite the dire state of the economy and the expectation of ferocious cuts in the autumn budget. There was a pent-up energy for wholesale reform in the department, and he was able to tap into it.

We, as his team, had to liaise with those officials and push them when he pushed us for results, so it was important that we got on with them, while still retaining a measure of political distance. 'If you need something done, tell them the minister wants it, even if he doesn't know about it,' was an insider's recommendation, which I sometimes followed. You also come to know that there are few secrets kept from the secretary general in the department. Problems or issues with the advisers or important information from other departments or agencies which officials learned about were conveyed pretty smartly to the top. Secretary generals hate to be caught napping or unaware of key developments, so they rightly insist on being kept in the loop. They need an internal alert system so that they can head off problems before or when they arise, and they need a plan in place to deal with them. They also have an early-warning system to tell the minister if some crisis is about to break.

There was, naturally, some unease about having a former journalist on the staff, one who had spent nearly all his working life trying to find out what was going on in education. Now, suddenly, I was on the inside. In my second week in the job, I had six reports on my desk which would all have been exclusive front-page lead stories in my previous life, but I couldn't do anything about them except treat them as confidential. After a while, officials began to realize it was useful to have a former education journalist as a special adviser who might alert them to the dangers of putting something in writing that could be FOIed, or who would spot something in a report that was crying out for a headline which might not suit the department. And that was before the finished product and draft press release went to Deirdre Grant.

Every Monday at 1 p.m., all the special advisers met in the Sycamore Room in Government Buildings to review items on the Cabinet's agenda for the next day. The chairing of the meetings alternated between the Taoiseach's and the Tánaiste's chief advisers. In the beginning, we used to thrash out other major news stories of the day as well, but that practice soon fell by the wayside, and the joke became how many elephants in the room would not be discussed, even if the nation was talking about nothing else. On a number of occasions, Seán MacCártaigh, a former journalist and short-lived special adviser to arts minister Jimmy Deenihan (Fine Gael), succeeded in getting us to turn around and at least consider those elephants. But when he returned to the Arts Council, from whence he came, it was Cabinet agenda business as usual, and little else besides. After one meeting, a fellow adviser turned to me and said, 'Not a word about turf-cutters or DEIS [disadvantaged schools]', the two big issues of the day, as far as the media and ministers were concerned. It got to the ridiculous stage where the ministers' special advisers failed to have post mortems on major political events such as budgets, or the election of Michael D. Higgins as president, or the defeat in October 2011 of the proposed constitutional amendment that would have allowed the Houses of the Oireachtas to conduct full inquiries into matters of public importance. A rare post mortem did take place after the government got a pasting for its initial mealy-mouthed response to the release of Martin McAleese's report into the state's involvement with the Magdalene Laundries system in

February 2013. We concluded that we should have discussed the handling of the report and the likely reaction the week before.

The ostensible reasons for not discussing the hot issues of the day were because they were not on the usually lengthy Cabinet agenda, which we had to preview, and because everybody was under pressure to get back to their respective offices. Advisers had to explain to colleagues what a particular item on the Cabinet agenda in their area entailed. Was it a memorandum for information or for decision by the Cabinet? What were the implications, particularly for other ministers who would have to be alerted to any potential landmines? And, if it was a contentious report or decision, how was it going to be handled for the media?

Most of the memos and reports were already up on eCabinet, the secure intranet system accessible to ministers, advisers and senior officials, all of whom had their own password. The secrecy was stretched a little when individual memos were circulated within departments, which had to respond by preparing either a 'no observation' response for their minister, or one listing observations they wanted. The 'obs' were drafted by officials, the advisers looked at them and suggested tweaking where necessary and the minister signed off on them. That was the theory, anyway, but sometimes, under the pressure of deadlines, the advisers would sign off on behalf of the minister, especially if the obs were not contentious.

As items and memos on the Cabinet agenda were sometimes leaked to the *Sunday Business Post*, a handful were deliberately kept back until the last minute. This was done for good reason on occasion, as premature disclosure could cause serious problems, particularly if the matter involved secret information from the Department of Finance. Minister Michael Noonan's adviser quipped at one meeting about the Cabinet that the next day his minister would be 'bringing in a memo underarm, but not underhand'. Other times, advisers would say that their minister – usually James Reilly – planned to circulate a late memo that Monday afternoon, a practice that spread, and infuriated the Taoiseach's and Tánaiste's offices, as it meant little or no time to debate the political implications. Finally, an exasperated Kenny said no longer, except in a real emergency, would late memos be taken at Cabinet meetings. They would have to be circulated for observations in plenty of time if they were just the normal 'urgent' business. In government, all business is urgent.

Now and then, the 'ordinary' special advisers such as myself would get wind of the horse-trading that goes on in the top echelons of any coalition government. We weren't part of it directly but would hear about it if a row delayed some particularly contentious memos. The Taoiseach's people and the Tánaiste's team would do deals to allow the other side to get a contentious memo through, provided they got one of theirs through too. Or else some memos could be delayed for leverage by the Taoiseach's or Tánaiste's people. This was done either to gain time to thrash out details of a proposed decision that would cause problems for the other side, or because the timing didn't suit one or other side, or simply because relations had plummeted for some reason over something a minister said, or somebody had leaked some information. The horse-trading didn't always work, such as when, to Labour's fury, Fine Gael insisted that Phil Hogan's heavily flagged memo on water charges would stay on the Cabinet agenda and be discussed before the May 2014 elections. The Tánaiste's people wanted it pulled until after the election. But that's part of the rough and tumble of politics and gambling.

As the months wore on, it became increasingly obvious that more and more issues were being discussed at a higher level between the Taoiseach's and the Tánaiste's people, who steadily acquired more and more power and influence. The fact that they were on the secretive Economic Management Council (EMC) added to their growing authority. The EMC – comprising the Taoiseach and Tánaiste, as well as the two finance ministers Michael Noonan and Brendan Howlin, their main advisers and a few key civil servants – took the final key decisions on the first budget later in the year, and Joan Burton made little secret of her annoyance that it bypassed the Cabinet.

The meetings concluded with the special advisers listing any forthcoming important announcements. Not everybody contributed as openly as they should, but I did at first, in the belief they should all know what was coming up, good and bad. Sometimes this caused me grief from the Fine Gael side, which asked too many awkward questions, and sometimes from the Labour side, which felt I was giving too much away. Some advisers would contribute little or nothing at this stage, and the first their colleagues heard about a major policy announcement or a report from their department was from the media, which seemed to me a short-sighted approach. 'Treat them like mushrooms,' a Labour aide suggested, semi-seriously, while Ronan O'Brien, Brendan Howlin's witty special adviser, suggested I was becoming 'the best boy in class'. I got the message, so I reined myself in, but I continued to flag some of the more important issues in education coming down the tracks.

After the special advisers' meetings, I would alert my

colleagues in the department if there was something new coming up the next day of which we had not been aware. Ruairi wouldn't get too upset about things popping up in other departments at the last minute, as he knew that was the nature of government.

While he was easy to get on with, I quickly realized that Ruairi was the last person in the world you would go into on a Monday morning and say, 'Jeez, that was a great match yesterday.' He got bored easily and simply didn't do small talk, especially about the weather. At his weekly to-do meetings with the team, he would sneak a surreptitious glance at his watch after about forty minutes, and you knew the rest of the agenda would be rattled through in double-quick time. The face of his watch was always on the underside of his wrist, which made it easier to check. Sometimes, he would quite openly look at it to get the message through to long-winded delegations. And the requests for meetings with him were endless.

He decreed early on that he wouldn't meet delegations about school buildings. In the past, local representatives had made a big deal of arranging to meet the minister of the day about a badly needed school-building project. When they were accompanied by members of the local Vocational Education Committees (VECs), it cost the taxpayers money for travel and subsistence allowances. He said simply that there was to be no queue-jumping and there was no point in having time-wasting meetings to satisfy local TDs and senators when the answer would still be the same – take your place in the queue – and he introduced much more transparency, with every project going up on the Net on the department's website for all to see. In no time, Neil Ward grew to relish the job of dealing with TDs and senators who were constantly making political representations about school buildings, teaching and special-needs-assistant (SNA) posts, and so on. He got to the comfortable stage with them where he could tell them to get lost when necessary, sometimes in pretty strong terms.

While he could be impatient, Ruairi rarely got really angry. But he did get exasperated with officials on occasion over their sense of time, which he felt was different from his. He conveyed this impatience either directly through phoning the key official involved and asking for progress, or through us. On one occasion he did fly into an absolute rage over something very silly said on radio by a spokesperson for one of the department's satellite agencies – the 'colonies', as I dubbed them – that deal with services to schools and colleges, teachers and the education system generally. 'Are you going to ring them or am I?' he said between clenched lips. An old friend of his had once advised me, 'When he gets angry and wants to bawl somebody out of it, remember to calibrate what he says.' Unfortunately, on that occasion, I didn't follow this sound advice and I conveyed his exact words, as instructed, much to the spokesperson's upset. Afterwards, I was sorry I hadn't waited and talked to him again when he had calmed down before making that phone call. It was one of the few occasions he really lived up to his caricature as Mr Angry from Sandymount.

3. Poacher-turned-gamekeeper

An early decision Ruairi, and indeed the department, had to take was whether or not to allow in a film crew to make a 'fly-on-the-wall' documentary. We agreed to it, and over four months film-maker Adrian McCarthy and his team got unprecedented access to meetings between the minister and advisers, and between the minister and department officials, across-the-table discussions between the minister and his officials and representatives of school management, and so on. Entitled 'Inside the Department', it was well produced and shown twice on RTÉ, though its first transmission was up against the first episode of the revived *Dallas*. From the viewing figures, it was clear that people were more interested in the doings of fictional Texan oil barons than in how policies on their children's schooling were playing out. The film crew had shot two hundred hours of footage, so most of it went on the cutting-room floor. Only after the programme went out on air did I tell Adrian how glad I was that one meeting of Ruairi and the team hadn't made the cut – the one where, as the camera was rolling, I realized that Ruairi, Neil, Ian and I were all wearing white shirts and red ties. Had it aired, we would have looked like members of a show-band!

As a former newspaper man, I knew how easily even small things could capture the media and then the public's imagination. Watching for banana skins – whether trivial or serious – and getting out the message were constant challenges for the department's hard-working press office. It was an eye-opener to see how things worked from the inside. A bought-in service provided the daily list of education-related news stories and those in which Ruairi was mentioned, and it was usually a very long list. But it was surpassed on a weekly basis by the stories from the provincial papers about education: huge numbers of them – stories about school openings, presentations of certificates, achievements, VEC meetings, and so on. Sometimes they carried wildly exaggerated claims from local opposition TDs or other public representatives. When the future of small schools was a big issue, Ruairi Quinn must surely have closed every one of the country's nearly 3,200 primary schools at least twice, such was the level of hyperbole that appeared in the provincial press. As a former journalist, what disappointed me was that it was only on very few occasions that the local media would check with the press officer to find out if Ruairi really intended to close the schools in question. The reality is that fewer than half a dozen schools close annually, and that didn't change at all when he was in office.

Over my years in journalism I had noticed that education ministers reacted in different ways to stories in the media. Some got very angry. One refused to talk to me for six weeks after I wrote something she didn't like. Her press officer refused to take my calls for ages. Noel Dempsey bawled me out of it when I mentioned his son, who was in a private third-level college in Dublin – and he was right. But Paddy Cooney, who was Fine Gael Minister for Education from February 1986 to March 1987, was very sanguine about them. Once, a major story appeared on the front page of the sadly defunct *Sunday Press* with a screaming headline that would be hard to miss. I rang Cooney's home at lunchtime, apologized for doing so on a Sunday and asked him for his reaction to it. I could hear him sucking on his pipe, before replying, 'Sean [he always called me that], to tell you the truth, I've only read the sports pages so far.'

Ruairi read the papers and everything else you put in front of him avidly. He couldn't but have been pleased with a soft-focus interview the press officer had arranged for him in the *Sunday Independent* magazine early on. There were nice pictures and easy copy but little revealing about the real man, who can be very private. Adrian, the documentary maker, told me he also found it hard to discover the man behind the politician.

While he would go along with a feature interview like this, Ruairi hated having to do some of the glad-handing stuff that accompanies politics. You rarely saw him photographed on the stump kissing babies or grannies, but he could do so if required. He also wouldn't do gimmicky 'photo-ops', as they're called. Without even consulting him, I turned down a request for him to don a wig for a Fun Hair Day event in schools for charity. As he is even more follicularly challenged than I am, I couldn't imagine him with a wig, even for a good cause. His colourful ties were his concession to making a statement. Once, when asked why he had such an array of them, he responded by saying that, with a face like his, he had to do something to draw attention elsewhere. (The ties became a bit of a thing. Before we arrived at one conference in Letterkenny, we were told later that a flustered and tieless general secretary of the Irish Vocational Education Association, Michael Moriarty, had rushed into a men's shop nearby saying, 'Quick, quick, give me a Ruairi Quinn tie.')

Ruairi got annoyed sometimes over inaccuracies in education stories and was amazed when the *Irish Independent* in the autumn of 2011 had no fewer than three front-page lead stories about a maths 'crisis' (to do with the variable quality of maths teaching at second level and the alleged lack of qualifications of a significant number of maths teachers). He got upset for his family over stories that started in the *Mail on Sunday* in February 2012 about mileage claims for his car.

Ministers usually have two drivers, often former gardaí, who can be trusted for their road skills, their ability to handle situations such as protests if necessary and their discretion. Many's the confidential conversation they've overheard, either over the minister's mobile or between the minister and advisers on their way somewhere. As a cost-saving exercise, and to make better use of gardaí, the traditional pool of garda drivers for ministers was replaced by a system whereby ministers hired and paid their own drivers and claimed mileage. The impression given in the *Mail on Sunday* story was that Ruairí was milking the system, and that hurt. Fellow minister Leo Varadkar had started putting his expenses up online for all to see, and, if anything, his mileage was slightly higher than his fellow Dublin-based colleague Ruairí, but he wasn't being targeted.

The *Mail on Sunday* stories by Ken Foxe did hasten the planned introduction of a new system whereby part of the annual mileage was ascribed to ministerial personal usage and was not claimed for. Ken, dubbed the 'keyboard warrior' by some or 'that fucker Foxe' by others around Leinster House, got most of his information through the FOI requests, a route he had used to great success in 2009 in the *Sunday Tribune* by revealing the high costs incurred by former Fianna Fáil minister John O'Donoghue on travel, hotels, car hire, the use of the government jet, and so on.

Other journalists use the more traditional route – the leak.

Now, the grand conspiratorial leak is a rare enough occurrence. Apart from official reports, briefings and events, other stories are usually compiled from titbits of information gathered via off-the-record chats over the phone or a coffee, or in a snatched meeting, and if you're lucky you might get sight of a confidential paper or report. If you're even luckier, you'll have your own private 'Deep Throat'. When I was education editor in the *Indo*, I had a long-standing contact who was head of an educational organization that rarely made the news, which was exactly as he wanted it. But many confidential documents would pass his desk which he knew were newsworthy. He would ring me on my mobile and say, 'Hey, Walshe, I'm surprised you haven't written about . . .' and mention the subject of the day, and then he would ask, 'How did you miss that?' I would have to confess I didn't know about it and go through the ritual pleading for a look at whatever document or new report he had acquired, which he would finally agree to. He knew the source of the story would never be revealed and gleefully joined the chorus of condemnation of the leak the next day if it caused the expected ructions.

Also from my days on the education beat – this time with the *Irish Times* – I have the distinction of possibly receiving the only solicitor's letter Charles Haughey ever sent to a journalist, despite all that was written about him before the truth came out about his finances. The letter demanded a 'correction and apology' for a story of mine about the sale of the former teacher-training college Carysfort College. I had written about his involvement in the deal, which saw University College Dublin getting money from the Department of Education that was used to buy Carysfort from businessman Pino Harris. Harris had earlier purchased it in the hope that

it could be converted into an international college for students, especially from the Middle East, but quickly realized
he had bought a pig in a poke and needed to offload it, as the
maintenance bills were rising rapidly. It can be safely said that
he was most grateful for the dig-out from the state. Haughey,
then Taoiseach, wasn't happy with the stories I was writing,
and his letter was seen as an attempt at a 'gagging writ'. I'm
glad to say he never got the apology.

Most, but not all, of the national political stories in the media
are written or broadcast by the political staff who inhabit the
same goldfish bowl as the ministers and politicians: Leinster
House. If they get it wrong, or too right at the wrong time, it
can disturb the dynamic between them and the sources
whom they have to nurture, and, in the words of one correspondent, 'You don't piss off your sources.' But sometimes
they do, because they have misunderstood something or the
headline overstates the story.

Journalists in general can also be too demanding. Now
that I was on the other side, I was taken aback to discover
quite how strong was some journalists' sense of entitlement
to immediate attention, with an accompanying readiness to
take offence or detect a slight if they didn't get what they
wanted when they wanted it. Expressions such as 'I need an
answer before noon' or 'I have a deadline' were used all too
often by journalists, who rarely thought just how busy other
people, including press officers, were. In fairness, with the
proliferation of media outlets and the constant demands for
updates, staying on top of things led to a kind of feeding
frenzy among journalists.

As I mentioned in the last chapter, early on in the job I
had half a dozen potentially great stories sitting on my office
desk which I could do nothing with. I made the mental

switch from being a poacher to being a gamekeeper immediately I took up the position of adviser. I felt I had to prove my trustworthiness to my new colleagues in the department by demonstrating that I wouldn't leak any information. The political reporters soon gave up ringing me and asking for a 'steer' on something from other departments, knowing that I had access on eCabinet to confidential papers. I made it clear that I was not going to be a 'source' or even 'a very reliable source'. But I did enjoy walking through town on crisp winter mornings, budget secrets and other confidential documents under my arm, running into hacks who would have loved to get their hands on them and simply not giving it a thought.

That ability to keep schtum stayed with me to the final moments. So when RTÉ's Sean O'Rourke was pursuing me the day Ruairi resigned, I had no problem ignoring his texts. Sean and I go back a long way – we were both brought up in Galway, are both graduates of NUI Galway and we sometimes play bad golf together – and I had encouraged him to go into journalism. When I apologized to him later, once my job was over, it wasn't just for that, but for having prevented an interview with Ruairi about the latest junior-cycle developments some months previously. It would not have suited us at the time to have him on air. My apology to Sean was for ignoring his texts, not for doing my job: though I had spent most of my working life trying to get stories into the media, as a ministerial adviser I had to spend part of my time trying to keep at least some of them out.

As an outsider who became an insider (albeit for a short time), I was far from being alone. The Houses of the Oireachtas were home to many former journalists who had jumped to the other side of the fence and never left. Some began to relish the sense of being at the centre of where real decisions were made, and it seemed they could never go back. James Reilly's press officer in health was Mark Costigan, a former political correspondent with Today FM. Passing Minister Reilly's office, you would always see Mark with an earpiece attached to a mobile phone which was constantly busy. Mark was generally liked by journalists, but he wouldn't let them get away with errors. Mark had a tough beat in health, which was too often in the media for the wrong reasons. He once told his minister, 'You're in danger of becoming addicted to the daily crisis.' I met him in Kildare Street on one particularly bad day which had brought new problems for his minister, and remarked on it. He gave me a variation of his previous boss Mary Harney's famous line about a bad day in government being better than a good day in opposition by saying, 'I'd rather be in the middle of a problem than be in the middle of nothing.'

So why do politicians leak gossip, information or reports, or allow their press officers or advisers to do so? Often, it's to get their view across through 'sources close to the minister', or it might be to send a warning shot across some other politician's bow, or it might have no immediate benefit other than for a grateful journalist to say, 'I owe you one.'

Sometimes it could be just for sheer devilment. I did it myself once when I drew the *Irish Times*'s Miriam Lord's attention to a Dáil question asked by Fianna Fáil Westmeath Longford TD Robert Troy, who wanted to know if the minister would consider giving CAO points to Leaving Certificate students for keeping fit. Now, Robert, opposition spokesperson on children, is, like most other people, naturally concerned about obesity in society, but trying to measure fitness levels for points purposes is simply daft. As Miriam asked in her Saturday column, 'What next, points for getting up in the morning?'

Speaking of Miriam, Miriam Lord-proofing speeches in advance was always good practice, for she has a knack for spotting political humbug and sending it up mercilessly. So, for example, when I noticed this line in a draft speech – 'We must support each other as we embrace change together' – destined for delivery by Ruairi at the teacher conferences, where we could hardly expect to be warmly embraced, it quickly got the chop.

Miriam also has a pretty finely tuned sense of the ridiculous. She – along with like-minded former colleagues such as Lise Hand – would have loved the story of how, in May 2012, there wasn't a sinner in the entire Department of Education and Skills or, even worse, in the Department of Foreign Affairs, able to read a document in French. Neil had managed to get a draft EU document related to the Stability Treaty ahead of it being officially conveyed to the government. The problem was that it was in French and we couldn't figure out how important it really was. Ruairi had a reasonable smattering of the language, but not enough to read it with accuracy. There was nobody available in the Department of Foreign Affairs either, as they had reduced the number of translators to save money. We had to send it to the Irish embassy in Paris to get it translated. As the French might say, '*Incroyable!*' (Another 'you-couldn't-make-it-up' story of the sort the media loves was when the Teaching Council – the body that promotes professional standards in teaching – made a mess of the ballot papers for election of members to the council and, on legal advice, had to run the elections again. Two typos – cost: €200,000. Somehow, the story didn't make the leap from some commentary on education blogs to the mainstream media.)

Of course, you can't always save a minister from himself. We were lucky that Ruairi was savvier than many, but even he put his foot in it occasionally. He was mad keen on the use of technology in schools but didn't always understand the terminology. In the Dáil in October 2012, he said that the introduction of fibre broadband in second-level schools would mean they had capacity of 2,000 megabits per second. No TD or journalist spotted how superduper such a speed is – twenty times faster than schools were being granted. However, he wasn't as bad as the other prominent minister in the same Cabinet, whose first lesson in computers had him putting the mouse on the computer screen when he was told to use it to move the cursor.

Journalists might sometimes wonder if their stories have any impact on politicians or government departments, or are simply absorbed by the system and overlooked. They're not overlooked, and they do have an effect on the politicians and on the civil servants. In one revealing entry for 2011, Ruairi wrote in his diary that 'The constant attacks by the *Independent* daily seem to be having some kind of impact, not personally but on troops and supporters.' Ruairi read the teacher and *Irish Times* columnist Breda O'Brien religiously, if that's the word. Even though she was a social conservative, and they would probably have disagreed fundamentally on many issues, he had a high regard for her. On one or two occasions, I can recall him being disappointed when she strongly attacked his plans for the future of Catholic schools.

As an adviser, what surprised me was the barrage of so many issues every day and how the system responded to stories in the media. There was often a request for an explanatory note for the Taoiseach's office in case he was asked about something in the media during Leaders' Questions in the Dáil Chamber. This provides leaders of the opposition with an opportunity to ask the Taoiseach or the Tánaiste of the country virtually any question about any issue, serious or not. Many questions were predictable, and notes were prepared in advance about the major issues floating around. But his advisers had to listen to RTÉ's early-morning 'It Says in the Papers' for any unexpected stories they had not anticipated. Then it was a quick read of the papers, followed by a phone call to an official or fellow adviser to get the necessary information for the note.

The opposition more often than not took the main story in the *Indo* and asked something based on it, for example, 'Is the Taoiseach aware how people are hurting because of his government's decision to cut such and such a grant?' The Tánaiste took Leaders' Questions on Thursday, and Eamon Gilmore's people sometimes went to ridiculous lengths to cover every possible question, with packed meetings late on Wednesday evening and early Thursday morning to discuss what could come up. At one such meeting I was at, there were seven or eight of us getting in the way of each other and of quick decisions on what notes were really necessary. On the few occasions Ruairi had to step in to take Leaders' Questions in Eamon's absence, he was much more relaxed about it, and generally winged it pretty well without masses of paper in front of him. He also cut back on the length of Dáil replies prepared by officials who used to get into a flap when it was his turn for parliamentary questions (PQs) every few weeks. They produced reams of supplementary information just in case it was needed, but it was largely a waste of their time. Ruairi decreed that, in general, answers to oral questions should be no more than 150 words, and if he did not know the answer to a supplementary he would simply tell the deputy he would send it on. It generally worked.

PQs often provide a handy story for journalists, particularly the education correspondents. The media interest in educational issues is relentless. When I was education editor with the *Irish Independent*, my colleagues from overseas were constantly surprised at the huge space devoted to education in the Irish media. It's largely because of the huge interest parents take in the education of their children. Its importance is deeply ingrained in the Irish psyche. Parents see it as the way for their children to better themselves. For decades, in rural Ireland, it was the only option for those who would not inherit the land. In the cities, particularly in the capital, qualifications are seen as essential because of the competition for jobs. The percentage of young people who remain in the school system to the end and go on to third-level education is among the highest in Europe.

Ruairi was well aware of all this and knew that there would be huge media interest in the controversial areas he was going to tackle. They touched on such hot potatoes as Church–state relations, fee-paying schools, class sizes, reforming the Junior Cert and funding higher education. These battles were all ahead of us.

4. The corridors of power

The door from the Ministerial Corridor in Leinster House to the Department of the Taoiseach is the most important door in Government Buildings, and entry can only be gained through it with a special white key card. Issuing of the cards is carefully controlled. Ministers have them, obviously; staff working on the far side of the door also. The others are shared between senior advisers and private secretaries. The late Fianna Fáil minister and my old schoolfriend Seamus Brennan famously told the Greens when they entered coalition with Fianna Fáil, 'You're playing senior hurling now, lads.' Indeed, through that door is where the senior hurling and many of the All Irelands are played. Not only is it the home of the Taoiseach, but on the far side of that door are flights of corridors holding the offices of some of the most influential and unknown – and unelected – movers and shakers at the top of Irish government. It is where the Cabinet committees meet, it's where the special advisers meet, and it's where the secretive EMC holds its sessions in camera, mainly about budgetary issues.

When I was attending meetings there, I usually went in through the main gate of Leinster House on Kildare Street, through the foyer, down the corridor on the right, up the main stairs, along a passageway at the side of the Dáil Chamber and over a bridge to the Ministerial Corridor, which has that door leading into the Department of the Taoiseach. If I wasn't going to see Ruairi, I would usually ask his private secretary, Ronnie Ryan, for his swipe card, which would allow me to go through the magic door.

On the right on the way in was the office of Martin Fraser, secretary general to the Taoiseach and also secretary general to the government. He always seemed to be in the right place at the right time. It is a hugely important post. In the relatively early days of the coalition, in July 2011, Fraser replaced the somewhat socially conservative Dermot McCarthy, who had held the post for a turbulent decade. Towards the end of his time in office, McCarthy had assumed an almost God-like stature of authority and gravitas. He happened to be in the Department of Education and Skills on one occasion when we were trying to resolve a particularly difficult problem over the successor organization to FÁS. He was prevailed upon to offer his advice. He had become somewhat more corpulent since I had first met him many years earlier. The physical change in him only added to his air of importance. That day, he sat at the end of the table in the secretary general's office, sphinx-like, listening almost impassively, and then offered sage advice, which we acted on with his help.

Further down the second-floor corridor is the Sycamore Room, which has a fine oblong table made of sycamore. Apart from the Cabinet meeting room, it's probably the most significant venue in the corridors of power and is used for a variety of meetings, including those with ambassadors and official delegations.

The Sycamore Room is the venue for the monthly Cabinet committee meetings that deal with social, economic and health issues, and so on, and are attended by the relevant ministers, their officials and advisers. It was at these meetings that I really got to see Enda Kenny's management style at close quarters. Ministers came and went, depending on what topic was being discussed. Often, you would see individual ministers hanging around outside in the corridor before they went in, chatting to each other or their advisers, or on the phone. The Taoiseach's chairing of the meetings was brisk and businesslike. More often than not, he was good-humoured, even funny at times. He would frequently adopt a folksy approach to particularly thorny issues, along the lines of 'Last week I met a farmer . . .', or it could be a business-man in Crossmolina or a teacher in Ballina, and this person would be giving out about a particular difficulty he or she was having with some arm of the public service. Usually, the nub of the story was why was there so much red tape restrict-ing ordinary people who were trying to go about their daily lives and better themselves.

When there was a long, tiring, intense series of meetings during the day, his attention would start to waver and he was less taxing on officials. I watched one day as an official from another department, which had clearly made a mess of acquiring a building much needed for a particular public ser-vice, got away with it when asked to explain what had happened. He looked at the Taoiseach and, in that way in which some civil servants can spin fine-sounding words out of thin air, said, 'Well, Taoiseach, it's an evolving situation,' as if that explained the cock-up. The Taoiseach accepted it and it was on to the next piece of business.

In the early days of the coalition, the Cabinet committee meetings were spread over different days of the week. But the Taoiseach got annoyed on one occasion in January 2013 when not a single Dublin minister turned up for a committee meeting on a Monday to discuss the Pathways to Work plans, while he had left Mayo on Sunday to be there. If he had known they weren't coming, he said, he could have stayed at home and come up on Monday in plenty of time for Tuesday's Cabinet meeting. He made his displeasure known by getting Martin Fraser to ring the offices of the Dublin ministers, including the departments of Richard Bruton, Joan Burton and Ruairi Quinn, to let them know. He decreed that, in future, all Cabinet committee meetings would be held on the first Monday of the month and would run through the day. As Pat Rabbitte remarked after he had left government, the Taoiseach is no Bambi.

Next door to the Sycamore Room is the office of the Taoiseach's chief adviser, Andrew McDowell. He was regarded as something of a right-wing ideologue and for being intellectually articulate in negotiations. But you would hate to play poker with him, as he keeps his cards very close to his chest. He's a descendant of Eoin MacNeill, the Minister for Finance in the first Dáil, and grew up in a staunch Fine Gael family in Donnybrook, Dublin. His influence is hard to understate and was graphically illustrated by an entry in Ruairi's diary in December 2012, when he wrote that 'the Labour Ministers were told that the government could collapse because of the intransigence of Fine Gael, who are dominated by Andrew McDowell.' Still, if getting on with your opposite number is an essential component of the chemistry that makes coalition work, McDowell did try very hard with Gilmore's economic adviser Colm O'Reardon.

A couple of doors further down the corridor was the office of a bright, younger adviser, Paul O'Brien, whose shiny good looks, dark-framed glasses and slick black hair prompted a prominent Fine Gael Minister of State to nickname him Clark Kent. Others – on the Labour side – dubbed him 'Sebastian' because of his debonair, public-schoolboy attitude, straight out of the eighties television series *Brides-head Revisited*. At the end of the corridor was another adviser, Angela Flanagan, with whom I had a fair number of – mostly courteous – dealings over three years. A bit proper betimes, she reported directly to Andrew and, like him, she gave very little away.

Another key figure in the Taoiseach's department was his chief of staff, Mark Kennelly. The Kerry native and long-term political survivor might leave the higher-order thinking and arguments to Andrew McDowell, but he was no slouch when it came to hand-to-hand political battles. He kept a close eye on the backbenchers, often priming ministers on what line to take, both in public and in private. He feared, or at least pretended to fear, Ruairi's agenda for divesting Catholic schools and would lob in an 'Are ye trying to take down the crucifixes from the schools now?'-type probing and poking question when I went in to talk to him about something else. He put you on the back foot straightaway, and I would end up jabbering about Ruairi being a pluralist, not a secularist. Once you're talking like that, you're losing, as he knew right well. I remember him turning around to me at one Cabinet committee meeting, when the future of small primary schools was on the agenda, and saying, 'Is this another one of yer mad fecking ideas?' (The truth was that the report which prompted the discussion had been commissioned by Fianna Fáil's Mary Coughlan when she was Minister for Education and Skills.)

Kennelly spent at least some of his time on what the public might regard as trivial issues but which are important to politicians. On one occasion, I was called into a meeting to meet the two Marks – Kennelly and his counterpart in Labour, Mark Garrett. And what was so urgent? I thought.

The country was still down the tubes financially, we were facing international opprobrium over the abortion issue following the death of Savita Halappanavar in Galway, where, it appeared, she had been refused a termination of her pregnancy that was needed to save her life, and the social-welfare cuts were going to be awful. Yet three of us who, between us, were paid €400,000 annually (they got more than me, of course) to help save the country could spend half an hour discussing board appointments to education bodies. As I tramped up and down the corridors of power, I sometimes wondered about political priorities.

Fine Gael generally insisted on its two-thirds share, Labour got the other third. In theory, the names were supposed to come mainly from the list of applicants who went to the trouble of putting their CVs online to the Public Appointments Service. This was part of the coalition's drive for more openness and transparency. In practice, some don't come through that route. If the chosen ones had been encouraged to put in an application in time, so much the better; if not, there was no problem. The bottom line was that many were appointed – still are – because of their party links. Increasingly, however, people were being appointed without remuneration or, if there was payment, they were encouraged to forgo it.

A constant visitor to the offices of Mark Kennelly and Andrew McDowell was Feargal Purcell, the Fine Gael-appointed government press secretary, whose office was on the ground floor. Purcell rapidly became renowned among his colleagues for his colourful metaphors. 'The only way to go through a red herring is with positivity,' he once told us at a special advisers' meeting. When the conservative libertarian Declan Ganley, founder of Libertas, championed the 'no' side in the European Fiscal Compact referendum, which was carried, Feargal remarked that Ganley had 'hoped to jump on a trampoline but instead jumped into a bog'. On the eve of a Sinn Féin weekend Ard Fheis, he predicted that, in terms of publicity, 'We will cover them like a cheap suit.' On another occasion, after Ruairi was lambasted at a couple of teacher conferences, he sent an unintentionally hilarious text message to Deirdre Grant, saying, 'Chin up, chest out, truth and accuracy will out.' But for all the poking fun at his mixing of metaphors, even his harshest critics agree that he has helped Fine Gael successfully champion the 'jobs, jobs, jobs' mantra and message, much to Labour's chagrin.

At the end of the Fine Gael corridor was the magnificent wood-panelled Taoiseach's office, a worthy office for the prime minister of a republic and a fitting venue for receiving distinguished visitors from overseas, some of whose photographs adorned the walls. All around the office were gifts from heads of state and other dignitaries.

Some Labour people joked that the Blueys, as they are usually referred to, adopted an 'upstairs downstairs' attitude towards the smaller party in the coalition. In fact, at that time the Tánaiste's advisers were all upstairs, along yet another corridor, one where the floorboards creak. First on the left was Colm O'Reardon's office. O'Reardon is an Oxford economics Ph.D. graduate and brother of Labour TD Aodhán Ó Ríordáin. Colm had the appearance of an intellectual bouncer; he could be mercurial, and demanded high standards of those around him. He didn't look at you directly when he argued, and when he wanted to finish a difficult discussion he had a most unusual gesture: he would put his arms straight out in front of him, with his palms facing you – as if to push you away – and say, 'Listen, what we are going to do is . . .' or 'What you guys need to do is . . .' His body language certainly made you realize who was in control of the discussion and its conclusion. Eamon's other special adviser was Jean O'Mahony, a TCD graduate who played an important part in the negotiations leading up to the forma-tion of the government. She was young but had a good old-fashioned social democratic belief in the power of the state to shape policies that would help the lives of struggling families and the disadvantaged. I was to have a lot of deal-ings with her as well.

Opposite Jean's office was that of Mark Garrett, the Tánaiste's chief of staff. Protecting his boss was obviously his priority. He tore strips off us on one occasion for not alerting the Tánaiste's office to a contentious report on special-needs pupils which was being released on a Thursday morning when Eamon was taking Leaders' Questions. He has a PR background, having worked with the Competition Authority and for the influential management consultancy firm McKinsey in New York, and it showed. Although I was not a member of the Labour Party, I went to the party's annual conference in my home town of Galway in April 2012 and saw him in operation. He masterminded the appearance for the televised leader's address on the Saturday night. There is nothing worse than RTÉ cutting into the middle of a speech and saying, 'And there we have to leave it.' There was no danger of that on this occasion. Garrett looked like one of those airport signalling staff guiding a plane to safety on the ground, and he gave Eamon extravagant arm signals to indicate how much time he had left and when he had to finish. He ensured that his leader finished in time and that the inevitable standing ovation also went out live. (Despite his efforts, there was only so much Garrett could control: an aggressive protest outside received as much publicity as the party proceedings inside. And the double whammy came when the maverick Galway East TD Colm Keaveney beat Galway West's TD Derek Nolan and former Waterford TD Brian O'Shea for the chair of the party. I knew Keaveney well from his student-politics days in USI, and even I could see he would not be an acquiescent chair or easy to control. Up to his resignation two years later and his subsequent joining of Fianna Fáil – 'A match made in heaven,' quipped Pat Rabbitte – Keaveney would cause the Tánaiste and Garrett endless headaches.)

Garrett worked closely with Cathy Madden, the Labour-appointed deputy government press secretary. In my diary, I described her as a 'whippet-thin redhead, talks in sharp bursts, phone constantly ringing, looks like your stereotypical PR woman from hectic PR company, always looking for the "line" to take on whatever the issue is, married to Danny McConnell from *Sindo* [the *Sunday Independent*]'. She has since been replaced by another Paul O'Brien, a former *Examiner* journalist.

The various people who worked in or frequented offices on these corridors, along with ministers and members of both parliamentary parties, were to play an important part in Ruairi's reform agenda. They contributed to progress and setbacks on a number of fronts, including thorny issues such as fee-paying schools, a proposed capital-assets test for deciding who should get higher-education grants and the future of small primary schools (which will be looked at in later chapters).

Ruairi knew that a lot of what he was proposing would be met with opposition from the wonderfully named 'partners' – both those in government and those in education. He had a full agenda, and it was always doubtful that we would get everything to the floor of the House, even if he were to stay the full term and survive a Cabinet reshuffle.

I recall the junior minister in education, Ciarán Cannon, looking shell-shocked after we'd briefed him on two contentious issues that were on Ruairi's reform agenda. He said that if one (the future of small schools) was a hand grenade, then the other (a proposed capital-assets test for families of those entering third-level education) was Hiroshima. That, I realized, was how politicians saw things: in terms of the level of political fallout they could anticipate.

Education is a political issue, after all. I remember reading a comment made after a heated Dáil debate years ago – 'Nothing moved the House like the debate on education.' Those who think education should somehow be removed from politics are mistaken. Do that, and you won't get many rows, but you won't get much money either. Just ask ministers in charge of departments that are further down the pecking order of importance and priorities.

5. Getting the bishops onside

Shortly after I was appointed, a bishop asked me, 'What are you working for that atheist for anyway?' I suggested to my episcopal interlocutor that he should be careful what he wished for, as the worst development from the Catholic Church's point of view was a minister who had no interest in religion. Ruairi had never made any secret of his atheism, but he had an unusual interest in the place of religion in society. At one lunch in Leinster House, I was bemused by the lengthy discussion between him and two priests about the controversial Swiss theologian Hans Küng, among others. (I was also bemused by the wording of an introductory message drafted on his behalf to DES staff. 'I was blessed to get the job I always wanted,' it read. Fortunately, I got the word 'blessed' changed in time.)

When it came to setting up the promised forum to look at the patronage of Ireland's primary schools, Ruairi was a man of his word. The launch was scheduled for Tuesday, 19 April, less than six weeks after he had taken up office. And at least one Walshe had a role in the success of the day – my grandson, Cian. Indirectly, he helped ensure that a key player, the Archbishop of Dublin, Diarmuid Martin, was present at the launch – an important endorsement of a process that was seen as being highly sensitive, in terms of Church–state relations.

The rationale for the forum was simple. Irish society had changed dramatically, but the patronage of primary schools had not. In the 1961 census, the 1,107 people who declared themselves as of no religion were literally a footnote in the published returns from the Central Statistics Office. Fifty years later, that figure had risen to a quarter of a million, while the numbers who were in the 'non-stated' category rose from 5,625 to almost 70,000 over the same period.

Yes, there were some more multi-denominational schools to cater for an increasingly diverse society, but thirty-five years after the opening of the first such school in Dalkey, County Dublin, there were still fewer than seventy under the patronage of Educate Together, compared with around three thousand under the patronage of the Roman Catholic Church. This meant that parents in most parts of the country had no choice about where to send their children to school. Even if it was desirable, the state couldn't afford a parallel system of multi- or non-denominational schools, so the way forward was obvious – get the Church to hand over some of its school buildings to other patrons where there was a clear parental demand for change.

This wasn't as radical an idea as it sounds. In Dublin, the archdiocese had already made disused buildings available to Educate Together for a couple of multi-denominational schools. In fact, I discovered later from the archbishop that he was planning his own surveys to test opinion in some areas, such as Ballyfermot, to see if the parents felt that an existing local Catholic primary school should be transferred. Ballyfermot was mentioned as it has a largely settled population and a good number of Catholic schools. Diarmuid Martin had gone on record as saying that 90 per cent of Dublin primary schools were under his control for about 50 per cent of the population who actively wanted a Catholic education.

Shortly after the invitations to the forum launch had been issued, I discovered that Diarmuid Martin had not been invited. The reason given by the official dealing with the list was that the invitations had gone to the bishops and it was up to them to decide who should come. This was *Hamlet* without the prince or, in this case, a prince of the Church.

Enter my four-year-old grandson. I'm not sure who said that small children and dogs are a great way to open a conversation, but Cian was my introduction to Diarmuid Martin when our paths crossed ten days before the forum launch. Nearly every Saturday, Cian and I go shopping in Bray – the butcher's, the supermarket, the spice shop, Gusto Italiano's on the Quinsboro Road, where I get a cappuccino and Cian gets his 'hot chocolate, but not too hot', and, lastly, Cormac Redmond's Get Fresh greengrocer's next door. The forum list of invitees was on my mind that morning when I spotted the archbishop walking up the road towards us. He was on his way to the Church of the Holy Redeemer on Main Street for a confirmation ceremony and had a few minutes to spare. I introduced Cian to him, reminded him that I was friendly with his cousin in Galway, Leonard Martin, and then I mentioned that I was now working with Ruairi and would love to talk to him about the forum. He told me to ring his office on Monday and he would clear a space in the afternoon. Then, after another friendly word with Cian, he was off.

That Monday's pilgrimage to his office proved to be worthwhile. My mission was to try to convince the archbishop to come to the launch. Ruairi's driver, Seamus Cosgrove, wasn't exceptionally busy that morning, so he drove me out to Drumcondra. Archbishop's House is not only the residence of the Archbishop of Dublin but also a complex of offices from which the archdiocese is administered. In the old days, the house was referred to as the Archbishop's Palace. But the house Seamus drove me up to could not be described as palatial; it was just a fine sturdy old building set well back from the road leading out to Dublin airport. I was received by the archbishop's secretary, Monsignor Paul Callan, who led me into a reception room which had a couple of comfortable enough chairs around a small table. I sat on the wrong one, as the archbishop remarked, 'I usually sit there,' when he came in a few minutes later. I moved to the opposite seat. We had an hour-long discussion over coffee, talking about religion and education, particularly the future of Catholic schools in a changing society. He struck me as somebody we could do business with. He was willing to try to push for divestment of some schools to provide real choice but was clear that he wanted the remaining Catholic schools to be very Catholic with their religious symbols and Catholic teaching. Then we came to the crunch – would he come to the launch of the forum? I argued that if he didn't it would appear that either he had snubbed us or we had snubbed him over the invitation and the media would have a field day. It would be, in the jargon, 'a great story' if he wasn't there. After all, he had said he had too many schools under his patronage and was one of the first to call for a forum on patronage. He's pretty media savvy and could see how the story would play out, so he agreed to come, much to my personal delight. A very pleased Ruairi noted in his diary that 'John Walshe has certainly earned his spurs. Diarmuid Martin is coming.'

The arrangements for the forum were now right, but the mood music had become a problem because of some discordant notes struck by Ruairi. He harped on publicly about Diarmuid Martin's 50 per cent figure too much, creating the impression that a row was brewing and that he wouldn't settle for anything less. Setting the bar high might be a good opening gambit in negotiations, but I realized he had gone too far when one journalist rang up and said he was writing a piece stating as a fact that half the country's schools were being handed over by the Catholic Church the following January. I explained that was incorrect, that all we hoped was that the process of handing over schools would actually begin the following year and we accepted that it would take a long time. I told Ruairi he was frightening the horses: his rhetoric might appeal to many in the Labour Party, but if he came across as too hard line, the Church would play the long game – wait until he was gone and then cut some kind of deal with his successor.

By that stage, Ruairi had realized himself that he was causing a problem, as his diary entry for Thursday, 7 April, notes that he has got himself 'into that place of confrontation with the Catholic Church between Church and state over control of schools and religion and education'. The same day, Sean Flynn reported in the *Irish Times* that the Church would not give up control of primary schools easily. 'Fr Michael Drumm, chairman of the Catholic Schools Partnership, said change needed to be thought through carefully. Critically, he also raised the prospect that only 10 per cent of schools may eventually be transferred – well short of the 50 per cent target raised by the minister.' Then a story appeared in the *Sunday Independent*, suggesting that there would be a confrontation between the minister and the archbishop at the forum. I convinced Ruairi to take a vow of silence on the 50 per cent figure, which he did for most of the following three years. But the characterization of him demanding 50 per cent of all Catholic schools stuck.

The launch took place in the Clock Tower building in the department's complex in Marlborough Street. The archbishop arrived on the day, with minutes to spare before the forum started. There was no confrontation. Rather, he and

Ruairi had a brief, friendly and very public exchange. Ruairi later described him as 'an Italian diplomat with an Irish accent', a reference to his many years at a senior level in the Vatican. Far from there being a row, they clearly hit it off from the beginning, and in subsequent encounters.

The launch was a triumph for the chair of the forum, Professor John Coolahan, Ireland's education treasure. He made a thoughtful and generous speech, as befitted a distinguished educational historian and former professor of education at NUI Maynooth. Johnny, as he is universally known, has been central to the formulation of national education policy for decades. Ministers of all political hue, south and north of the border, have asked him either to chair education groups or write reports, which are invariably sound and well received. When she was Minister for Education, Fianna Fáil's Mary O'Rourke asked him to join the team writing her revised Green Paper after she reacted strongly to a draft that had been prepared by her officials. She took a boat trip near her home to read the officials' version and recalled later, 'I was tempted to toss every single page into the waves of the Shannon. It seemed to me that caution had spancelled everything.' Most recently, Johnny was responsible for a report on the future of teacher education in Northern Ireland. He also has a huge stock in the OECD education division, as I was reminded on my own brief stints writing, editing or contributing to reports there over four hot summers in Paris.

In his address, Johnny reminded the audience that Ireland had established a distinctive consultative tradition for education policy and said this forum would be a continuation of that long and successful tradition. 'We have a good track record in using our collective wisdom to come up with acceptable solutions on, at times, complex issues on which there are varying viewpoints,' he said. And he talked about the importance, in moving to 'a balance of rights', for 'mutual understanding of positions, an acceptance of different stake-holders' bona fides, a respect for divergence of viewpoint, an empathy for varying perspectives, and a reaching out with a sense of generosity to reach compromise and best possible solutions'.

The launch attracted good publicity, but then the hard work began. Whatever his views about Ruairi's exuberance over the 50 per cent figure creating difficulties, Johnny never contemplated abandoning the forum task, such is his commitment to public service. He worked well with the two other members of the advisory group, Dr Caroline Hussey, former UCD registrar and Labour Party stalwart, and Fionnuala Kilfeather, former CEO of the National Parents Council (Primary) and a person very concerned about the human rights of non-believers. Submissions were sought, and the main groups – parents, managers, patrons, unions – were invited to a Q and A session with the advisory group, which would probe their submissions in depth between 22 and 24 June. The sessions were open to the public and were streamed live.

The report was ready the following spring, sometime before the teachers' conferences. At the suggestion of Mark Garrett, we released it during conference week, when education dominates the airwaves and attracts acres of newspaper space. The reason it does so is two-fold. The first is that there's not a lot else happening; the courts and the Houses of the Oireachtas are on holiday and news is scarce. The second is the high level of public and media interest in educational matters. The three unions, who hold their conferences at the same time, know how the media work, and they release reports and surveys, trail issues, write and time speeches to get maximum coverage over that week. There is competition between them for the best coverage.

Some years ago, the Irish National Teachers' Organization (INTO) stole a march on the other unions, the Association of Secondary Teachers Ireland and the Teachers' Union of Ireland, by starting its congress with the presidential address on Easter Monday, instead of the more usual Easter Tuesday. That gave them a head-start in the publicity stakes. The INTO's press officer, Peter Mullan, is a dab hand at dealing with the media. He once quipped that he'd prefer it if the education correspondents didn't attend the INTO congress, as they tended to ask awkward questions and it was much easier to give a 'line' to younger, freelance reporters. But he knew how demanding covering the congresses is, with travel, listening to the radio to see what's happening at the other conferences, early deadlines for stories, opinion pieces and editorials, the inevitable late-night drinks with delegates to make or renew useful contacts, and so on. He introduced a system of runners to collect and photocopy speeches from delegate speakers which were then distributed to the grateful media.

But neither the media nor the unions were grateful to us for usurping their plans that week. Emma O'Kelly from RTÉ asked if we could postpone publication, as it made her travel and work plans more difficult. I refused. She did a piece on RTÉ suggesting we were trying to set the media agenda for the week. That was precisely what we were doing. And it worked: the forum report and Ruairi got massive publicity, even in the *Financial Times*.

We knew the main education partners would be asked for their reactions to it. There is nothing worse than being landed with a report and then asked to make a comment on air about it a few minutes later. The instinct is to respond to the newspapers' version of it, which might not be accurate or successful in capturing its nuances. For that reason, I had briefed some key education players in advance on the contents of the report.

This turned out to be fortunate, as an initial media report suggested, inaccurately, that we were trying to ban crucifixes in Catholic schools. From our point of view, it would have been disastrous if they had responded to that erroneous reporting. What the report actually said was that boards of management should develop a policy on the educational display of religious and non-religious artefacts and works of art in a school. Such displays ought not to be exclusive to any one faith or tradition but should have a balance, reflecting the beliefs of children attending the schools. This was a long way off banning crucifixes, but the initial inaccuracy went into the ether and caused us no end of problems.

Fr Michael Drumm did a good job on radio and was reassuring from the Catholic Church's point of view (including pointing out that we hadn't suggested removing crucifixes from schools). Drumm is the Church's go-to person on education. I would hate it if he were my supervisor for a postgraduate thesis – he is bursting with brains, as we used to say when I was growing up in Galway. He is also forensic, drilling down into documents and pointing out inconsistencies and mistakes. He spotted, for instance, that in the forty-seven areas listed by the department in a document published in 2010, Portmarnock and Malahide appeared twice in the lists of forty-three towns and four Dublin areas. Nobody had copped it before that. It was worthwhile briefing him in advance.

Despite the positive response to the forum report, there was caution – and even downright hostility – in some Church circles, doubtless due to fears about Labour's views and intentions. There was, of course, Ruairi's unwise early harping on about the 50 per cent figure. But the Catholic Church doesn't need an excuse to question Labour politicians' motives: it is naturally wary of Labour ministers because of their perceived social agenda in education and elsewhere. This is a long-standing issue: I remember a priest strongly criticizing Niamh Bhreathnach at a reception in the Gresham Hotel following the annual teachers' Mass in the Pro-Cathedral when she was the first Labour Minister for Education in the mid-1990s. This particular priest was an influential figure in the education world, and I was surprised at his misplaced anger towards Niamh as her draft education bill – subsequently enacted by Micheál Martin – legally enshrined the denominational nature of Catholic schools, which certainly satisfied the Church.

Many involved in Catholic education were still smarting over a document written by John Suttle and proposed by the Clontarf branch of the Labour Party in June 2011 entitled 'Illegal Religious Discrimination in Ireland'. The twenty-nine-page document argued that the Irish government was colluding in a breach of the constitution in funding national schools which discriminate on religious grounds. It claimed that 'Losses in religious vocations, scandals about child abuse [and] falling numbers attending religious services seem to have strengthened, rather than weakened, the Catholic Church's determination to maintain its dominant position in schools at both primary and second level.' Most controversially, it proposed that 'All senior appointments in state bodies which are likely to have to deal with the Catholic Church should be screened to ensure that they will not show inappropriate deference to the Catholic Church. Those who feel that they are "Catholic first and Irish second" should have no influence on the control of education.' The document, as Ruairi quipped, was not very subtle. In fact, it had been over-whelmingly rejected by two Labour conferences, but it still rankled with Church leaders.

The closure of Ireland's embassy in the Vatican by a Labour Minister for Foreign Affairs, Eamon Gilmore, in November 2011 probably confirmed the worst suspicions of those doubtful about Labour's motives. They did not buy the official line that it was a cost-saving exercise following a review of the economic return of overseas missions in strait-ened times. The closure was read as a calculated snub by the coalition government and a follow-up to Enda Kenny's sen-sational July attack on the Vatican in his Dáil speech reacting to the latest report on clerical sex abuse, this time concerning the diocese of Cloyne.

Neither was the debate about divesting helped by a series of articles in *The Furrow*, the journal published out of the Catholic seminary in Maynooth, that tore into the forum's recommendations. One of them, published in mid-2012, was a veritable call to religious arms. A lecturer in Mary Immacu-late College in Limerick began by predicting that if the forum proposals were implemented they would destroy the Catholic ethos in schools. 'Given the fact that the transmission of faith now mainly occurs in the schools rather than in families, this is effectively a recipe for the utter secularization of Ireland,' wrote theologian Rik Van Nieuwenhove. He concluded by saying that, in his view, 'Not one single Catholic school should be divested until we have cast-iron guarantees that a genuine Catholic identity will be maintained in stand-alone schools.' Stand-alone schools are those that are at least three kilome-tres from their nearest neighbour, and there are 1,700 of them in the country – mostly in rural areas.

A professor in the same department, Eamonn Conway, a priest in the Tuam archdiocese, was not quite as trenchant in his article, but the message was the same. The forum report was a cultural marker and a wake-up call, he suggested. 'It is difficult to read the report without concluding that "the inherited pattern of denominational school patronage" is considered to have no place in a modern society, an impression underlined by the detailed account given to the origins and history of the patronage system that portrays it as belonging to a different era,' he wrote. It was a surprising comment, given that the main author of the report, John Coolahan, was not only a recognized expert on the history of Irish education, but also chaired the governing body in St Patrick's College of Education, Drumcondra, the Dublin counterpart of Mary Immaculate College. Not a man to put a 'spin' on things to suit a political agenda.

Professor Conway also inferred that the report was suggesting that there would be no more schools under denominational patronage. (This was not the case at either primary or second level. Indeed, Ruairi Quinn was the first Minister for Education in thirty years to sanction a new Catholic second-level school – he ended up approving three of them, and one Protestant school, because that's what parents in the areas voted for in surveys he had introduced. Not bad for a secular atheist!)

The forum report gave us a road map ahead, and the reaction to it by more level-headed players on the Church side was encouraging. But, clearly, progressing matters was going to be far from straightforward, and getting the first Catholic school over the divestment line proved to be much more difficult and time-consuming than anybody could have anticipated.

6. Making the cuts

The annual budget set dance is like something out of Lanigan's Ball. Figures go in and out of the calculations – and in again and out again and round the houses and back again. The figures, and the 'budget measures' (as they are officially called), dance before your eyes on an endless supply of confidential papers. Possible cuts and spending increases appear, then disappear, then reappear again as some other options are dropped. The figures change as they are calculated and recalculated, and the tots keep changing – as does the gap you have to make up.

The pace, especially coming up to budget day itself, can be frenetic, as ministers from the big spending areas – social welfare, health, education, justice – have bilateral discussions with the minister and officials in the Department of Public Expenditure and Reform, DPER (or Diaper, as one DES wit dubbed it). The bilaterals usually come after an endless flow of papers and phone calls between officials and advisers on both sides.

And just when you think everything is in place and the press releases and speaking points for the minister can be finalized, the scene changes again, for entirely political reasons. This could be because of huge negative public reaction to a particular measure that has been leaked or floated, or it could be because it has gone down very badly with a focus group.

The budget was discussed continually at ministerial,

adviser and official level from shortly after Ruairi came into office right up, literally, to the last minute, when changes were being made or sought. It's difficult enough for a new government to prepare its first budget. And even more so when its ministers are out of practice. This was the case as we geared up for the budget in 2011. And not only had the ministers been out of government since 1997, but the government increased the pressure on itself by deciding to carry out a comprehensive review of expenditure for the next three years. In other words, the scale of the cuts coming down the tracks over the following years would also be revealed in December 2011. We were buried in a sea of numbers. Huge swathes of forest were sacrificed in circulating the calculations for that review.

The scale of the cuts for the first budget needed to be savage – the government had to save €3.6 billion. It had a massive Dáil majority and the public knew it was in for a tough time. There was some debate at government level then, and in subsequent budgets, between those who wanted a few big headline measures rather than political trauma by a thousand cuts. (Officially, they are savings in taxpayers' money, but to the media and opposition they are always 'cuts'.)

Ruairi realized early on that he would have to deliver considerable savings in his budget for his good friend Brendan Howlin. The department had to come up with savings of €76 million, to get the total departmental budget for the coming year down to €8.6 billion or so. Ruairi was used to preparing budgets, but it was new territory for his advisers. Of course, we knew how important it was. We also knew that every single pre-budget submission from the education partners would look for the one thing – more money – that was just not possible. Every representative body and lobby group is convinced that it is the most important organization. Whether representing the pre-school, primary, secondary or higher-education sectors, they all sing the same tune.

Hammering school transport and closing two of the four Roman Catholic colleges of education seemed to Ruairi two immediate possibilities to begin with. (As it transpired, neither made the cut.) He suggested that we, his advisers, should come up with our own ideas for savings. That proved to be much easier said than done, as the department's shopping list of possibilities already included everything, including our worst nightmare of cutting the miserable €4 a week meal allowance for FÁS trainees.

Ruairi knew that whatever choices were made, there would be trouble ahead, but wrote, 'I feel strangely liberated, as I will not be a candidate [for the next general election] and therefore am not scared, as I was in the past. Did Ray Mac-Sharry feel the same as he was heading for Brussels as a commissioner when he made his adjustments?'

Every department was under pressure, not just the big spenders. However, justice minister Alan Shatter had other ideas about what was required. Shatter arrived at his bilateral with Minister Brendan Howlin and the DPER officials not bearing gifts of cuts in his department but with the immortal words that he was there to address the 'historic financial deficit' in justice. This plea for more money was greeted with stunned silence. Subsequent retellings of the story were accompanied by hoots of laughter. Though Shatter was recognized for his hard work and dedication, he was regarded as aloof and was not the most popular kid on the block. (Bemusement with Shatter's unique way of going about things was constant. At a special advisers' meeting in December 2012, one senior person was heard to mutter, 'Oh, fuck!' when Shatter's adviser Tom Cooney said his minister was preparing a 'women's talent bank'. In time, when the government was under more pressure, bemusement turned to frustration.)

It wasn't just the forthcoming budget that was taking up so much time and energy, but the damn comprehensive review of expenditure as well. Officials were finding it harder and harder to find potential areas to cut without doing irreparable damage to the education system. Even the possibilities of worsening pupil–teacher ratios (PTRs) by drastic amounts and slashing student and a myriad other grants would still not yield the kind of savings DPER was talking about for the following two years. When the document was finally submitted to DPER, there were still gaps in the possible measures to make up required cuts in spending.

On 10 June, the transient nature of politics was brought home to one and all by the untimely death of the former Minister for Finance, Fianna Fáil's Brian Lenihan, who had stared into the financial abyss in September 2008. At the time, the government decided it had to prevent the collapse of the Irish banking system by guaranteeing all the banks, a decision opposed by Labour. Lenihan was universally well regarded, perhaps not always for his decisions but certainly for his general decency.

The euro crisis that was developing when Brian Lenihan was minister was growing steadily worse through 2011. As one of Ireland's true Europhiles, with a deep knowledge of and concern for European affairs, Ruairi was preoccupied by what it meant both for Ireland and for Europe. Having been Minister for Finance when the single European currency was named the euro, he was particularly concerned about its future. In his diaries, he reflected on his own involvement a decade and a half earlier in pushing through the concept and the euro name. In early October, he wrote: 'I have no regrets but my confidence is shook. The task now is can we fix it. That remains to be seen. I believe that we must and so we will.'

In mid-June, education's finance guru Michael Keogh had given us the first of many drafts on what the education budget would be like for 2012 – with strict enjoinders to the advisers to keep it confidential, not even to leave documents lying around on our desks when we were out of the office.

Although the officials prepared the documents, as advisers we had an input. Any final version would have to be signed off by Ruairi. Eamon Gilmore's advisers grilled Ian, Neil and me from time to time over what was being proposed by the officials in the department. It seemed to me that they accepted there had to be cuts, but somehow not ones that would hurt Labour supporters or constituencies – a near-impossibility in education. They wanted to protect disadvantaged young people on Youthreach, the education and training scheme for early school-leavers, and other programmes. They spoke in generalities such as 'No slicing or dicing' and 'Be creative' – whatever they meant. The one thing they were clear about was wanting to hit fee-paying schools hard, and they wanted us to get officials working on measures that would see such schools losing their government subvention over time, or at least a good proportion of it. Eamon's weren't the only advisers trying to protect their party's interests. The Taoiseach's people were pushing for big cuts, but preferably not in departments where they had ministers. It was the classic NIMBY approach.

There were so many versions of the proposals and the numbers flying around, it was sometimes hard to keep track of the changes, as they moved so fast. A few days after one meeting with Eamon's advisers, Colm O'Reardon bawled us out of it for apparently not taking on board suggestions they had made; these included protecting spending on Youthreach and on the National Adult Literacy Agency. He made it clear that if we wanted the Tánaiste's advisers' support for getting some concessions, then we had to do better. We had acted on their previous demands, which were accepted by the department but the protections were not in one of the many versions of the draft estimates that had been sent to the Tánaiste's office. We subsequently learned that Joan Burton's people received a similar grilling. It was clear that the Tánaiste's advisers were trying to politically proof the budget and reduce the potential fallout to the party as much as possible.

Ministers often talk about difficult choices, and there were endless discussions about where to find the €76 million in savings in education, especially knowing that even more savings would be needed the following year. Ruairi was well aware of the 'historic deficit' in spending on education – how its share of the public-spending cake had become smaller and smaller while health and social protection got bigger and bigger slices – so paring spending back so drastically was a tall order.

On top of that, it is all very well talking about cuts in education when you have a static or even declining pupil population, as is the case in many European countries, but we had to view things differently. The upward swing in our population had to be factored into our budget arithmetic.

Some months earlier, Ruairi had what he called his 'carcrash' moment when he realized the scale of the challenge ahead in providing places for the coming explosion in numbers. It came when he paid an overnight visit to the department's Building Unit in Tullamore, County Offaly. Officials in the department were forecasting an increase of over 45,050 primary pupils and 24,900 second-level pupils by the start of the 2017/18 school year, pushing total enrolments well over the 1 million mark. He was so alarmed by what was coming he felt he had to prepare a memo for the Cabinet to alert colleagues.

So, in June, he had announced that we were going to build twenty new primary schools and twenty new post-primary schools in the next six years. At the special advisers' meeting, I was flabbergasted when I was asked by another adviser if Ruairi had secured government approval for spending money to build and run the new schools. Strictly speaking, he hadn't, but what did the adviser want – a return to hedge-school days? We were in a difficult place financially, but a physical school place was still a basic right for all children.

All politics are, of course, local and, after the announcement of the new schools in June, Alan Shatter, through his adviser, enquired precisely where the promised schools in his constituency would be located. He wasn't at all happy when I couldn't tell him. I explained that if we identified the exact spot and word got out, then the owner of the land would shout 'Yippee!' and simply jack up the price of the property.

Apart from finding money for expanding enrolments and additional teachers, we also had to find extra money for initiatives such as Ruairi's literacy and numeracy strategy, which was planned by department chief inspector Harold Hislop, junior-cycle reform and the roll-out of broadband to all second-level schools, which had been agreed with Pat Rabbitte's Department of Communications, Energy and Natural Resources.

Given that almost 80 per cent of the education budget goes on salaries and pensions, in order to make savings there was no option but to look at staffing numbers and grants at primary, secondary and third level. The low-hanging fruit, such as additional posts for teachers of travellers or posts for English-language teaching for non-Irish pupils, had been plucked by the previous administration, so we had to climb higher to find something to prune back.

Various possibilities were discussed. One was a sharp reduction in the number of special-needs assistants (SNAs) which was heading towards the eleven thousand mark. The proposal was to cut this by 10 per cent or more, but this could be dynamite. Politicians are basically terrified of cutting special-needs spending, and it keeps on going up and up. All the opposition and the media have to do is point to the inevitable hardship case where a distraught family stands to lose education supports deemed necessary for their child. Such is the fear of those cases being publicized that it is easier for a government to cut higher-education spending and mainstream teaching jobs than it is to cut special-needs provision. The dilemma was that we were spending almost as much on special needs as we were on the underfunded higher education which the country relies on to produce the brainpower needed to drive the economy forward. But unless spending was checked, we might end up like some American states, where 25 per cent of the education budget is spent on special needs and higher education suffers even more.

The most difficult decision was what to do at second level – worsen the pupil–teacher ratio or bring guidance counsellors, and possibly chaplains, inside the normal quota of staff per school? Up to then, they were outside the quota and paid for by the state, including the chaplains in a large number of community schools and colleges. All second-level schools had an automatic right to either a part-time or full-time counsellor once they had a certain number of pupils. What was proposed was that, in future, schools would allocate guidance hours out of their normal quota of teachers and the ex-quota provision would be gone. The onus would now be on principals as managers to take the decisions on how best to use their overall teaching resources. According to some influential education figures we consulted on a confidential basis, this was the least-worst option, as it meant losing fewer teaching posts than if we changed the pupil–teacher ratio. But it was going to be controversial, and we knew the counsellors' best-known representative, Brian Mooney, would go wild in his *Irish Times* column. We opted for bringing the guidance counsellors inside the quota. As it transpired, it was not possible, for legal reasons, to do the same with chaplains.

Funding of fee-paying secondary schools was also back on the news agenda, following publicity given to a Dáil reply to a question from independent TD Maureen O'Sullivan, who was told that €12.3 million had been given in building grants to fee-paying schools over a number of years. Dáil questions about fee-paying schools had regularly been asked previously by Labour TDs, including Eamonn Maloney and Aodhán Ó Ríordáin. At that stage of the budget game, Labour backbenchers were baying for fee-paying schools' blood and wanted them pushed into the free-education scheme. At least Ruairi had taken them off the list for summer works grants, a scheme which helps schools pay for smaller jobs, such as rewiring or window replacements. But they were set up for a fall in the pupil–teacher ratio.

Higher education was also slated to take a big hit, or a

series of them. It was planned to reduce student maintenance grants by 3 per cent, while the student contribution
would increase by €250. It was proposed and subsequently
agreed that the means test for student maintenance grants
would be amended to take account of the value of certain
capital assets, as well as income. This was to be introduced in
the 2013/14 academic year, for new entrants.

Worse was to come, as scaling back the postgraduate
student-grant scheme and withdrawing maintenance grants
for new entrants starting in 2012/13 would save a huge
amount of money. The numbers staying in higher education were increasing significantly, partly because of rising
employer demands but also because more graduates were
remaining in higher education to ride out the recession. There
was concern in Labour over the impact of this measure on
those from very poor families, and some measure of relief
was planned for them. Later, Colm O'Reardon pushed for
the introduction of a loans scheme, which would help some.
We had discussions with the National Treasury Management
Agency and DPER about such a scheme, which one of the
commercial banks agreed to (though it charged a high interest rate, making this option prohibitive for many potential
students).

On top of all these drastic plans were cuts in day-to-day
spending at all levels. It was going to be tough medicine
indeed. By the end of October, Ruairi admitted to getting
'slightly anxious about the impact of the estimates and the
future programme on the capital side on third level'.

The nerves were not helped by the endless recalculations
of proposed measures. On a couple of occasions, something
approaching mild panic ensued when it was discovered that
officials had over-estimated potential savings from one

measure, while another had to be taken off the table after fears I raised about its legality proved correct. In Ruairi's absence on a particular day, Ian O'Mara and I had a couple of minutes to decide which unpalatable option he would agree to in order to save €5 million. Given that whatever option we recommended would mean reduced teaching hours for some non-permanent teachers, it was nerve-wracking stuff. It was particularly nerve-wracking as I knew that, though Ruairi was not one to throw around his weight, he was very conscious of whose job it was to advise and whose it was to make the decisions.

Brendan Howlin's adviser Ronan O'Brien had been chief adviser to Ruairi when he was party leader and had a soft spot for him, but neither he nor Howlin could spare education much. But O'Brien did ring me up late in the run-up to budget day with an offer of €5 million on the capital side – not a huge amount in the grand scheme of things but one that could be put to a lot of different uses. I suggested it could go some way towards a new law school in UCD, which was raising a considerable amount of private funding, particularly from former Attorney General and EU commissioner Peter Sutherland, but the university needed something from the state. Ronan wasn't too keen on the money going to train more lawyers when there were so many other urgent demands for capital spending at primary and secondary-school level, and said, 'Look, do you want this fucking €5 million or not?' We found a different use for it.

7. Leaking, kite-flying, spinning and U-turning

The leaking and the briefing before that first budget went on at a furious rate. The exercise served two purposes: one was to test public and political opinion and the other was to soften up the public. No matter what was proposed, you would get the inevitable pearl of wisdom to the effect that 'There'll be trouble over that one.' But when lots of different people said it, then it was time to listen.

Other big spenders were doing it, so we felt we also had to indulge in some leaking, as education would also be taking a major hit in the budget. 'We are preparing our backbenchers for the bad news, and I have my team working at it to minimize collateral damage,' Ruairi wrote. In mid-November, he had a good evening meeting with some Labour TDs and senators where – unlike Joan, who told them relatively little – he and Neil gave them a worrying indication of what to expect in the budget. Unfortunately, he undid some of the goodwill he had generated at a meeting of the Parliamentary Labour Party (PLP) the next day in a discussion about fee-paying schools, when he gave them a long history lesson about Protestant schools and their funding, taken mainly from a book written by my educational-historian namesake in TCD – not exactly what they wanted to hear. He wasn't able to attend a Labour central council meeting, so Neil and I went to outline Ruairi's reform plans and give some general indication of what was coming down the tracks. This was the same week that draft documents about the Irish budget were leaked in Germany and given to German MPs, revealing plans to increase VAT and cut expenditure and the numbers working in the public service as well as their pensions. Neil was much more used to the council members' company than a non-party member like me, so that day offered me a unique insight into what the grass-roots activists from around the country were thinking. Many were already deeply worried about the future of Labour, which was sliding in the opinion polls. There were the inevitable complaints from delegates about what was going wrong, but the negative and pessimistic tone of so many contributors, coming just nine months after an historic general-election win, was surprising. Eamon responded with a good, rousing speech, rounding on his critics, reminding everybody they had just won the presidency with their candidate, Michael D. Higgins, and a by-election in Dublin West with Patrick Nulty. It was easy to see that day why he had been elected leader of the party.

Meanwhile, the leaks were becoming a flood. The Sunday papers had the planned cut in children's welfare payments, and I thought, 'Somebody's doing their job getting that out there.' (Indeed, the leaking from health and social protection was so proficient that most of the measures planned by those departments came as no surprise when they were finally announced in the budget.) On Monday, 21 November, the *Star* gave two pages to the cuts expected in the number of special-needs assistants, but there was no pick-up elsewhere. Sean Flynn had the story in the *Irish Times* about the expected worsening of the pupil–teacher ratio at primary level. Stories about fee-paying schools being under threat were almost commonplace. I had played some part in these leaks, as we were doing much the same as other departments – trying to ensure that all of our possible cuts entered the public domain well in advance of the budget.

Labour national organizer David Leach was furious over a story I planted in the *Sunday Business Post* about moves to withdraw maintenance grants for those pursuing their studies at postgraduate level – an idea he was unaware of at the time. We had to make it clear to him that there was little option but to go ahead with the cut because of the significant savings it would yield, a point he reluctantly accepted.

The combined effects of the leaks were not just alarming the public. 'Frightened' was how David described the backbenchers at a Labour meeting, and with good reason. They were seriously upset by the possibility of a 10 per cent cut in children's allowances and by health minister James Reilly saying publicly he wanted to introduce a fifty-cent charge for medical card holders 'because of Brendan Howlin' – the implication being that it was all Howlin's doing, and somehow Labour's fault for not giving health more money. The reality was that DPER felt that Reilly had no real handle on health spending – the DPER view was known by politicians and by the media. The feeling in DPER was that it could pour billions more into health and the money would sink without trace. However, there was nervousness on the Fine Gael side over slashing health spending too much. Roscommon TD Denis Naughten had lost the Fine Gael party whip, having voted against the closure of the emergency department in Roscommon General Hospital in July, and they did not want any more ship-jumpers. There was also real fear in Labour that one or more TDs would jump if the budget was too severe.

Whatever was to happen about cuts in health and social protection, it was becoming abundantly clear that a cut in

SNAs was not a runner politically. Ruairi's secretary Denise Rogers sent a shiver through us all at one of our Monday to-do meetings when she suggested that cuts in SNAs would be Ruairi's 'medical-card moment', a reference to the previous government's plan to deprive the over-seventies of their automatic right to medical cards – an idea it was forced to shelve after a pensioners' revolt. She remembered, as did everybody involved in politics, when a hapless Minister of State, John Moloney, was booed and heckled and prevented from speaking in a crowded St Andrew's Church in Westland Row. Nearly two thousand people had turned up for a meeting in a local hotel, which couldn't take the unexpectedly large turnout, so they went to the church. They made it clear that they weren't taking it, and the government had to change tack. A consensus was arrived at in the department, and among the Tánaiste's team and the PLP, that SNAs could not be touched.

Dropping the proposal was all fine and dandy, but it meant we had to find savings elsewhere, which is never easy to do. Using the nuclear option of scrapping the school transport scheme altogether and perhaps replacing it with grants for needy families to make their own arrangements was mentioned regularly. It would have saved a lot of money but lost a lot of seats in the next election, as well as crippling Bus Éireann, which was paid to run the service on behalf of the state. It got plenty of airtime at various meetings, but Fine Gael would never buy it because it would lose them too many rural votes, so it was dropped.

Worsening the pupil–teacher ratio at primary level was an obvious option. We decided to adjust it from 28:1 to 30:1. So was making specific changes in the staff arrangements for small schools that would mean they would need a higher number of pupils to justify an additional teacher. And there were some 'legacy' posts remaining in disadvantaged schools which could, on paper at least, be phased out. These were additional teaching posts allocated under older schemes but not removed when a new scheme called DEIS – Delivering Equality in Schools – was introduced by Mary Hanafin when she was Minister for Education. Fianna Fáil was wise enough to let sleeping dogs – or, in this case, jobs – lie. We were shortly to discover that we should have done the same.

Back and forth everything went. Over and over again. Finally, we were into the home stretch. Three days before the budget, Ruairi's team was assembled for yet another collective run over the budget documents. Deirdre McDonnell, a career civil servant who replaced Deirdre Grant as press officer when she went on maternity leave, had done a fantastic job in preparing all the briefing documents, with Neil's political help. She knew the ropes, having worked as a multitasking special adviser to Fianna Fáil's Batt O'Keeffe when he was minister. After the meeting we had returned to our offices to tweak the final versions of the various documents when, unexpectedly, Ruairi called everybody into his office to announce that the Economic Management Council had taken the primary-school pupil–teacher ratio off the agenda. At a stroke, the EMC had destroyed the balance of cuts we had planned between the wealthiest and poorest schools and those in the middle. Ruairi later wrote in his diary, 'I survived a cut in primary PTR because the EMC decided to eliminate the proposal and fund the gap with taxation. Fine Gael used focus groups to test the kite-flying proposals and the primary PTR came back very strongly.' Focus groups probably were not the only people not wanting to rock the boat: the four politicians on the EMC comprised Eamon Gilmore and three former schoolteachers – Enda Kenny, Brendan Howlin and Michael Noonan. The U-turn would be a welcome decision for some, particularly in the INTO, one of the country's most effective lobbying machines. But it wreaked havoc elsewhere.

Brigid McManus insisted that Ruairi get Brendan Howlin on the phone and explain that this would leave us with an even bigger financial gap to fill in 2013. The original intention was to adjust the pupil–teacher ratio in 2012. Obviously, it couldn't be done in January 2012, for a very simple reason: the school year starts in September, so a reduction in January would cause chaos. The earliest the reduction in jobs could be implemented would be September 2012. This meant that the savings for 2012 would be only a third of a full year's savings, which we would get the following year. Brigid's concern was how would the financial gap be plugged in 2013? However, the argument fell on deaf ears, though we did secure some small alleviation of the ongoing moratorium on middle-management posts in schools. So much for the idea of making plans for three years; the government was still struggling to figure out Year 1 of the three-year plan.

More immediately, the EMC decision left us exposed over surplus legacy posts in disadvantaged schools. We had intended to exempt these schools from the general worsening of the pupil–teacher ratio but to make it clear that they would still lose their surplus legacy posts on a phased basis over the next few years. However, in the absence of change to the PTR – which would have caused a massive row – it meant that Ruairi's stated intention to phase out surplus posts in them stood out very sharply.

At the special advisers' meeting just before the budget, the Taoiseach's advisers said that the budget was about more than putting off financial Armageddon and we had to 'change the narrative' to that of being a reforming government. In other words, in the midst of all the cuts, real reforms in the public service and in job-creation measures were taking place. There was little or no discussion over the suggestion, as we were all under time pressure that day. I was asked to brief my colleagues on what to expect from education, and explained our measures. I was contacted afterwards by somebody on the Fine Gael side who asked if we could take the capital-assets plan off the table. This was the measure to include the value of certain capital assets as well as income in means tests for third-level maintenance grants. It was too late. It was already in the documentation for publication, having gone through the Cabinet without any major fuss, probably because there was so much to read and it had somehow slipped under the radar of the Taoiseach's advisers. Though it took a little while to ignite, this issue was to come back to haunt us.

Putting any kind of positive spin on what the government was doing was, to put it mildly, a big ask, and the sense of mounting crisis abroad didn't help. As the Greek financial crisis went from bad to worse, and attempts were made to mount a rescue deal, Ruairi wrote, 'My heart goes out to Greece and George Papandreou [the prime minister]. He is really struggling now and the whole euro could be at risk.' He became even more alarmed as it seemed that the euro problems were deepening and threatening to add to Ireland's difficulties. In early December, the week of the budget, he wrote: 'The impact of the euro crisis has got to me. Have I been deluding myself about my role? I keep thinking back to 1996 and 1997, but what could I have done otherwise? The relentless growth of cynicism and criticism of politicians and politics I find very corrosive.' A few days later, he returned to the topic: 'I look now in angst at the euro crisis and the posturing of Merkel and Sarkozy while remembering 1995–7. But I am getting less upset about it now and more sanguine.'

The budget for 2012 was effectively spread over two days, the first half, which dealt with the public-spending cuts, given by Brendan Howlin on 5 December, and the second part, dealing with tax measures and given by Michael Noonan, the following day. It was a daft way to do it, but not as barmy as the earlier suggestion of a wider gap of a few days between the two parts of the budget. In his press statement outlining the education measures, Ruairi said that there would be no increase in the general average of 28:1 for the allocation of classroom teachers at primary level. Tucked away in his statement, however, was an innocent-sounding measure: 'In order to ensure fairness in the distribution of resources available under the DEIS plan, it is no longer possible to allow some schools to retain legacy posts that pre-date the introduction of DEIS in 2005. Withdrawal of these posts will be done on a phased basis.'

On Wednesday, 7 December, Ruairi wrote, 'Well, the budget is through and we have had mixed reactions. The SP [social protection] measures on disability payments have stung badly and may now be ameliorated, as well as some CE [community employment] changes. There is a lot of hissing around a relatively mild budget, compared to the task that we have. We did meet our 8.6 per cent deficit target, and this is good. The Croke Park Agreement [on pay] is now very much in the frame.' He added that he would have to look at how to get savings from teachers' pay in order to keep them in jobs in the primary and secondary system. This was at a time when other front-line staff, such as nurses, were not always being replaced.

But the mixed reactions were about to be stirred up even more. We were beginning to hear noises, which grew louder and louder, over the decision to phase out the legacy posts. Political antennae were picking up backbench stirrings. In fairness, Ian O'Mara had always been the one to point out the political dangers of this measure. Aodhan Ó Ríordáin was first out of the traps and promptly organized a meeting with a number of principals and Dublin TDs, and got good publicity out of it. Not for nothing was Ó Ríordáin known in some quarters as 'Deputy Tabloid', such was his ability to get mileage out of the red-tops that are read by many of the voters in his Dublin North Central constituency. However, he had a legitimate interest in this issue, as he was a former teacher and principal of St Laurence O'Toole's Girls' Primary School. His very public stance would create considerable upset among other Labour politicians over the following few weeks, one of whom said, 'You'd think he's the only one of us that gives a fuck about poor people.' I never believed he would jump overboard, though: he was simply too ambitious. In his old school, his teaching colleagues, who were well aware of his political affiliations and ambitions, used to joke, 'Here comes the future Minister for Education.' He knew as well as anybody else that you can't do that much on the outside of government.

An initial modification of the proposals was worked out to ease the growing anger. On Thursday, 15 December, Ruairi wrote that 'We had a slight wobble on the education budget figures with the PLP, but due to good reconnaissance by Neil and Ian, and some expert help from Martin Hanevy [assistant secretary general of the department], we got it back on track and had the matter resolved by the PLP meeting at 7 p.m. yesterday.'

Ruairi was being over-optimistic in his mid-December assessment, and by the New Year the DEIS posts controversy had threatened to come off the rails entirely. 'Fasten your seat belts,' Ruairi told us as we settled back in after the Christmas break and prepared for private members' motions on disadvantaged schools from both Fianna Fáil and Sinn Féin, which would inevitably put pressure on the government, especially the Labour backbenchers.

What floored us was that a Labour Cabinet colleague joined the clamour. Minister Pat Rabbitte led a delegation of backbenchers to see Ruairi and demanded a reversal of the DEIS decision – a decision taken by a government of which he was a minister. Even PLP chairman Jack Wall, described at the time as an 'extreme moderate', was insisting that the decision be reversed and, unusually for him, banged the table at the same meeting to get his message across, something that was to become a more regular part of Jack's schtick as the government aged.

Rabbitte's extraordinary intervention and late-evening meeting with Ruairi in Leinster House was immediately revealed to the *Irish Times*, and not by our side. RTÉ was quoting backbenchers as saying that the decision would be reversed. What escaped the journalists were the unsubtle hints from some unelected people in the party that Ruairi's days as minister could be numbered if he did not sort out the problem and reverse the decision immediately.

The terror in Labour of losing backbenchers – or even senior figures – was very real. Junior minister Willie Penrose had gone in November, because of the closure of the army barracks in Mullingar. The following month, Dublin TD

Tommy Broughan lost the parliamentary Labour Party whip after voting to reject a government amendment to extend the state's guarantee of the banks for another year. Róisín Shortall, a former education spokesperson, and a junior minister in health, accosted Neil one day, accusing both him and Ruairi of a lack of understanding of working-class communities. There were fears that she would vote against the government and with the opposition motion. (She quit the following September because of disagreements with James Reilly.)

The fears of advisers and others were understandable, but their not so subtle threats to Ruairi's position were not very edifying. From their point of view, the pressure worked, and Ruairi was forced into a U-turn by announcing a cost–benefit analysis. And it was not the only U-turn, as Joan Burton had to back down on plans to delay disability allowances for sixteen- and seventeen-year-olds until they were eighteen, a move which had led to a public outcry.

Ruairi went on RTÉ's *Morning Ireland* and said simply that they were out of practice in government and had made mistakes. Writing in his diary, he was not bitter about it: 'The reversal of a budgetary decision is always a public admission of a mistake or the need to rethink something, and that is what I said this morning, in effect, on *Morning Ireland*. I will have to find the resources elsewhere in my budget allocation, but the numbers are not that big. The way it has been handled is a lesson for me for the future – get an impact analysis before a final decision is made.'

Mary O'Rourke rang me to say that his humility would wear well with the public. Humility may not have been her strongest point, but O'Rourke certainly knew the media and the public better than most – I always felt she would have been a journalist if she weren't a politician. And she was right. A few days later, Ruairi noted that 'My budgetary change and admission of a mistake have proven to be a big plus. I think that I can recover the lost ground with some enhanced authority, but I must combine it with a new display of steely determination.'

This sense of steely determination remained with him as he entered 2012. Early in January, he reminded himself that his chief objective – and his responsibility – was to be a reforming Minister for Education, and noted that he couldn't do anything about the euro crisis: 'What I can do is transform Irish education and that is now my driving focus and priority. This is the area that I control and for which I have a clear mandate and a Programme for Government.' A few days later, he wrote, 'The Troika return today. Our debt mountain rises and I continue to worry about our future and money in this little country of ours. Keep to the knitting!'

8. Progress comes, dropping slow

The report of the forum on patronage and pluralism in Ireland's primary schools had recommended surveys in a number of areas to ascertain the views of parents. In discussions with the Taoiseach's people, who took a huge interest in Church–state issues, one of the Taoiseach's advisers, Angela Flanagan, suggested a roadshow around the country where parents could get information and give their opinions to department officials. I knocked that one on the head, having too many memories of Minister Noel Dempsey's YES – Your Education System – series of meetings around the country in 2004 to ascertain parents' views. These quickly became hijacked by teachers, who used them as an opportunity to berate cuts in education spending and look for more money to be invested in the system.

However, there were problems with surveys. It sounds simple, but how do you ensure that a survey is transparent and objective? In the negotiations that followed with representatives of the Catholic Church, Educate Together and other patron bodies, the Church people suggested the questionnaires be handed out in school, but others objected that such a system could be open to abuse.

After some discussion, all the patrons and the department agreed that an online questionnaire would be made available to parents in five pilot survey areas in autumn 2012. But how do you prevent parents from anywhere in the country, not just the five selected areas, casting their preferences either for the status quo or for a change in patronage to an Educate Together multi-denominational school, or a *gaelscoil*, or one run by the local VEC? Indeed, how do you even know they are parents? The only valid way was by asking parents to give their PPS numbers, which could be checked with the Department of Social Protection to ensure they were genuine. Written questionnaires would be made available to anybody who sought them. In the event, few did.

There was a low response level to the online survey in the five pilot areas, and in the subsequent surveys the following year in thirty-eight other areas, and this allowed some in the Catholic Church to say that parents didn't want change. There were a number of reasons for the relatively low turnout. The fact that it was online put many people off, especially when they had to supply their PPS numbers. In terms of publicizing the surveys, the last thing anybody wanted was divisive town-hall-style meetings with clashes in local communities, so they were out. A code of conduct was therefore agreed which put a limit of €300 per patron in each area surveyed on advertising and promotional material by the various interested parties. The parents were basically asked which patron body did they want for their children's schooling. The choices were mainly schools under the patronage of the Roman Catholic Church, the Church of Ireland, Educate Together, the local VECs (later Education and Training Boards) and An Foras Pátrúnachta, which represented the all-Irish schools. In a small number of cases, other patrons or potential patrons put their names forward, including the Redeemed Christian Church of God, an evangelical group; the National Learning Network, which was linked to Rehab; and Lifeways Ireland, which represented the Steiner schools, of which there are two in County Clare. We tried to drum up some publicity in the local media but, in the jargon of journalists, the surveys were not a 'sexy' story and they didn't get much coverage, so many parents were unaware of them. Principals were not always eager to promote the surveys, especially if they saw a threat to the patronage arrangements for their school.

Despite this, there was sufficient interest in twenty-eight areas for a change of patronage of at least one local school, which the Catholic bishops, as patrons, were asked to pursue and then come back with specific proposals for change. But local objections and difficulties made for slow progress.

Arklow in County Wicklow is a good example. Despite Diarmuid Martin's stated views, the team he sent there to negotiate the possible handover of one of the half-dozen or so Catholic primary schools to Educate Together came back empty-handed. It was the NIMBY syndrome at its finest. Yes, we all agree that there should be choice and more multi-denominational schools, but 'Our parents are happy' was the response from each school approached. Overall in the town there might be sufficient demand for change, but that was made up of minorities in each school and the majorities did not want change.

While our dealings with the Catholic Church over school patronage were trying to break new ground, the government's overall relationship with the Church remained tentative after the Taoiseach's critical Dáil speech in July 2011. Ruairi rightly described the speech as historic in his diary: 'Enda Kenny, Fine Gael leader and practising Catholic, condemned the Vatican and the Pope in clear and damning language, making a break between Ireland and the Vatican in an unprecedented manner.' So it was with great anticipation that I went to a meeting between the Taoiseach, Ruairi, James

Reilly and children's minister Frances Fitzgerald, plus officials and advisers and the Catholic bishops in January 2013,
the first bilateral since the speech.

Now, here were the Taoiseach and his team, seated along
one side of the oblong table in the Sycamore Room, facing
Cardinal Brady on the other, accompanied by several bishops
and two priests. The discussion ranged over a number of
issues, including the North, the constitutional convention,
chaplains in hospitals and prisons, education, the closure of
the Irish embassy in the Vatican and, of course, the forthcoming legislation which would allow for abortion in very
limited circumstances. The Church side apologized to the
Taoiseach when he told them that he had been compared to
worse than Herod and asked where he would spend eternity.
Both sides were adamant on the abortion issue, with Cardinal Brady and his people talking about the holy book – the
Bible – while the government side talked about a different
book, the constitution.

I obviously had a particular interest in the discussion on
education, which began with five minutes *as Gaeilge* from
Brendan Kelly, Bishop of Achrony and head of the hierarchy's Education Council. Now I'd only ever heard Ruairi
utter four words of Irish, and that was when I put them in a
script for him the previous year. He didn't do the *cúpla focail*
at public events as some ministers did, in the pretence they
could speak the language. So I was bemused to see him nod-
ding his head from time to time as if following the bishop.

The government side revealed little after the meeting, but
we had to dampen down a story afterwards that the government had said it was looking again at the closure of the
Vatican. None of the government press officers was at the
meeting, and Cathy Madden contacted me urgently to see was

there anything to the story. All the Taoiseach had stated was that he noted the cardinal's views on it. But it was about to take off as a story, because somebody was spinning it that way for their own reasons. (As it transpired, the government did have second thoughts and decided to reopen it a year later.)

Progress on the divesting of schools did come, albeit slowly. It was somewhat ironic that after all the agonizing about how to get the hierarchy to play ball, the first Catholic school to be divested was not one where a bishop was patron but one owned previously by the Christian Brothers, who had transferred it to the Edmund Rice Schools Trust (ERST). The Brothers had relatively few primary schools, compared with the huge number of schools under the direct patronage of the bishops. History may be kinder to them than contemporary commentary. Like many of the congregations that have come in for heavy – and justified – criticism, the Christian Brothers' mission was admirable, and it educated tens of thousands of young males at little or no cost to the state when it couldn't afford it. However, the record of good work of the order was devastated by revelations of widespread abuse – emotional, physical or sexual, or all three – of boys who went through its schools and many of those unfortunate enough to have been sent to the residential institutions it ran. The state was already trying to get more money from the Brothers and seventeen other religious congregations to pay half of the staggering €1.4 billion cost of meeting redress compensation claims – to no avail, despite several meetings, letters and discussions. And now here it was asking ERST – which had taken over the Brothers' schools – just to give it a school building for nothing. A tall order.

The trust has a complicated structure of directors and

members, the latter including some of the big names in Irish education and society. The members' board is chaired by Mr Justice Peter Kelly and includes former MEP Pat Cox, former DCU president Dr Danny O'Hare, philanthropist Carmel Naughton and Professor Daire Keogh, president of St Patrick's College, Drumcondra, while the directors are chaired by the very diplomatic Pat Diggins, former head of the Education Centre in Drumcondra.

The negotiations with the directors and chief executive Gerry Bennett were tetchy. They were led on our side by assistant secretary general Kevin McCarthy, whose mild-mannered exterior belied the fact that he could be tough when necessary. I attended all of the meetings on behalf of Ruairi, who had more than a passing interest in the outcome. Indeed, all the main players, particularly on the Church side, were watching what was happening, as this was in the nature of a test case. The forum had suggested the transfer of divested schools on a cost-neutral basis. If the state handed over money to ERST for the property, every other patron would insist on the same, despite the tens of millions of punts and euro that had been poured into the schools over the decades. But the trust was looking for compensation to help secure its future.

The building in question was in Basin Lane in Dublin 8, where the Brothers had first opened a school in 1820. The current school was being amalgamated with another because of declining enrolments in the area. Educate Together wanted the site, but the deadline slipped by without agreement and it had to open in temporary quarters on Harcourt Street, but we still wanted the Basin Lane site for a permanent school. A compromise was reached after some months whereby, crucially, no money changed hands. The trust agreed to hand the school over, rent free, for a ten-year period. After that period negotiations would take place on an annual rent to be paid by the state to the trust. If the trust instead decided to sell the property at that stage, its debts to the state for capital grants etc. would be written off. But the assumption was that the school would remain available to the department (and thus Educate Together), which would then have to pay some rent. Call it kicking the can down the road if you will, but it was a reasonable deal all round. The key thing was that the state now had control of the property.

The other main element of the forum's recommendation dealt with small stand-alone schools and how the 1,700 of them could become more inclusive. They are almost entirely Catholic, and it was always going to be a challenge to come up with guidelines that suggested a way forward but without alienating the Church patrons whose goodwill was being sought to make them work.

Ruairi wanted a report out before he left office, probably in the autumn of 2014. When political developments brought his departure timetable forward, he put pressure on officials and advisers to come up with a document as soon as possible. It was a tight deadline, and they were used to his impatience to get things done and assumed he wanted it finished in case he left office sooner than expected.

The original intention in the Programme for Government had been to publish a White Paper on pluralism and patronage. That had been in Labour's election manifesto. The promise to publish a White Paper had seemed a good idea at the time, but such papers traditionally spell out firm government decisions and were not suitable in this instance, where the purpose was to give guidance rather than instructions to schools to deal with an evolving situation. In other words, the paper could not be prescriptive, but should be supportive, drawing on examples of good practice.

It was known that the Catholic Church was working on its own document on inclusive schools, but this would not be available until the autumn, at the earliest. At the INTO congress in Easter 2014, Ruairi criticized the Church for not giving the department the promised examples of where Catholic schools had proven to be inclusive and from which lessons could be learned about what works and what doesn't. It did a couple of months later, and four were visited in time for the finalization of a report which contained proposals to make the schools more inclusive. I went to three of the four schools to get a flavour of what was going on so I could assist with the preparation of the report by two officials under the direction of assistant secretary general Ruth Carmody.

Language in school policies is always important, especially where they are dealing with parents from overseas who are not used to Irish cultural mores and the way we don't always say what we mean, or where there's an apparent inconsistency between what's written down and what actually happens in practice (usually because those running schools are responsive to the realities on the ground). For example, in one school department officials and I visited as part of the exploratory exercise, the language in the school's policy was clearly contradicted by the practice. The policy was almost dogmatic in emphasizing the school's Catholic ethos, apparently to the exclusion of honouring important events in the calendar of other religions. Yet the school was clearly welcoming of pupils of other faiths, and of none, and had a sacred space in each classroom where all faiths were honoured.

The report looked at other issues, such as the scheduling of religion classes, the celebration of religious festivals and the display of religious artefacts, where once again the canard that Ruairi Quinn and his department wanted to ban certain artefacts – crucifixes come to mind – had to be dealt with. The report stressed the need for good communications with parents, an obvious point, but communication has to be two ways. The days of school authorities laying down the law to parents are coming to an end.

Talking off the record to some Church people, it was easy to pick up an attitude of 'We'll bide our time. This fellow will be gone shortly and things will be OK again.' But they won't, as society is changing dramatically and the school system has to change as well. Others in the Church know this and realize that the best hope for the future of Catholic schools is to reduce their numbers significantly.

It's hardly a secret that Diarmuid Martin is not universally loved by all his peers and some of his own priests, who sometimes see him as the darling of the Dublin media. What may not be appreciated is how deeply wedded he is to very strongly identified Catholic schools, complete with artefacts and symbols catering for the children of practising Catholics who want a denominational education for their children because they are believers. As he told a conference in Galway in April 2014, 'I am a firm believer in the value of Catholic schools and the Catholic school system, but I believe for that system to work and to be able to provide authentic Catholic religious education, it requires that there be a viable, accessible and tested system of alternatives which make real the choice of parents who wish a different ethos. It may seem a paradox, but the longer the Church exercises a near-monopoly in primary education, the more difficult it will be to foster and maintain a genuine Catholic ethos in those schools.'

The report was finished within a tight deadline and was

aptly called 'Progress to Date and Future Directions', as it could report some progress since the original forum report in 2011. Apart from Basin Lane, a number of schools are starting elsewhere in temporary quarters while talks are continuing on divesting local Catholic schools. There was an unexpected bonus in Mayo, when the local Church of Ireland bishop agreed to divest the Church of Ireland national school in Ballina to allow it to be taken over by Educate Together. Some will feel progress is not fast enough, either in terms of divestment or in making all schools, not just stand-alone schools, more inclusive.

Ireland has been criticized by the various international monitoring bodies for the mismatch between the number of multi- or non-denominational schools available and the rights of citizens in a more culturally and religiously diverse society. A UN report published in December 2011 noted the concern of other UN member states about Ireland's education system and called on Ireland to 'accelerate efforts in establishing a national network of schools that guarantee equality of access to children, irrespective of their religious, cultural or social background' and also to 'encourage diversity and tolerance of other faiths and beliefs in the education system'. Further reports from international bodies are expected to take a similar and increasingly tough line with Ireland.

The rights of parents who are non-believers or have minority beliefs are written into international treaties and conventions. They are also enshrined in the constitution. These instruments recognize the right to freedom of religion and belief. Ireland is a party to these treaties and conventions. The possibility is that an individual parent will decide enough time has lapsed and go to the courts to ensure that their acknowledged rights are honoured. It took decades for parents with special-needs children to wrest educational rights from the state through the courts. Indeed, the state treated these children and their parents disgracefully for far too long. It would be a pity if some parents become so frustrated that they feel they have no option but to go to court on the question of pluralist education too.

There are hopeful signs, however, that the message is getting through. The Progress Report got through the Cabinet on 1 July 2014 without any difficulty and was published that day. It attracted some but not massive amounts of publicity, partly because it didn't contain a great degree of the controversy the media thrives on and partly because there were plenty of other stories around. The next day, Ruairi announced his departure from office.

An unexpected and little noticed press release was issued the same day, 2 July, by the Bishops' Council for Education. In it, the bishops welcomed Ruairi's report, which, they said, would be helpful in sharing good practices across the system. It agreed with the report's finding that no 'one-size-fits-all' approach would work and that the best way forward was based on principles such as good communication, clarity in rights and responsibilities, openness to dialogue, and flexibility. 'Such principles have informed the dialogue between the DES and Catholic patrons to date. We look forward to continuing such an approach as the partners work together to reconfigure the education system so that it responds to the various social and demographic changes in Irish society.'

In many ways, the statement was remarkable. Who would have thought three years earlier that the Catholic bishops would issue such a welcoming statement about a report on religion in schools issued by the first openly atheist Minister for Education?

9. Slowing down the points race

It was too good an opportunity to miss. There we were, in April 2011, Ruairi, senior department officials and myself on the far side of the table from the seven university presidents, talking about the urgent need for change in the points system. Ruairi expressed his alarm at the massive growth in CAO course options, which had doubled in a decade. He wanted them to come up with proposals to reduce that number. The problem was, he didn't set a timescale. Knowing the universities and how long they would take to reach a consensus, I decided to intervene. Realizing what a privileged position I was in, I leaned across the table and said to them that what the minister would really like to see were proposals for change from them by September. One or two were clearly taken aback at the nerve of this upstart who used to write stories about them and was now suddenly telling them what to do. But I had settled into the job and, crucially, I knew I had Ruairi's backing. He was on a reform roll, having come into office just a few weeks earlier. So I was confident they would have to say yes – they would respond positively.

Looking for change and actually getting it are two different things, but change was desperately needed – just ask any student or parent who has gone through the January ritual of filling out the CAO form to apply for a college place. The Central Applications Office was founded in 1976 to process university applications centrally, and the first students to go through the system took up their places in autumn 1978. To streamline and centralize a previously disjointed system, the universities decided to make offers to Leaving Certificate applicants based on their exam results, with grades being allocated a points value that would be added up to make a total. The points per course depended on supply and demand for places. Thus the points race, as the late *Irish Times* journalist Christina Murphy dubbed it, was born.

Initially, the CAO acted only on behalf of the universities, but in the early nineties it was expanded to include colleges of education and regional technical colleges (the precursors to the institutes of technology). Since the mid-nineties, some private or partially publicly funded third-level colleges have also used its services.

The application form is straightforward. In the old written-form days, the CAO regularly wrote back asking applicants with names such as Sean or Michael if they really were female, as the box they had ticked suggested, or were they actually born on the day they filled in the form and not seventeen or eighteen years earlier. Most applicants now fill it in online and it is almost fool-proof. But, over the years, one part of the form became increasingly difficult to complete – which courses did students want to study?

Look up courses in computing or engineering on the CAO website and you're met with a bewildering array of options. Now, ask a teenager who is doing the most important exam of their lives next June what's the difference, for instance, between courses in computing with software development, or with multi-media, or with mobile app development, or with games development, in the Institute of Technology, Tralee. These courses are available at level 7, which is an ordinary degree, or level 8, which is an honours degree. Go figure. Or maybe they want to do engineering in DCU, where they have ten courses to choose between. Apart from the usual civil and electronic engineering choices, they can also opt for mechanical and manufacturing engineering or, my favourite, mechatronic engineering.

Ruairi was genuinely surprised when I gave him an early memo showing the exponential growth in the number of third-level courses. 'Did nobody call stop?' he asked when he saw that the number of CAO courses had trebled in the previous twenty years and applicants now had to choose from more than 1,300 options – around 900 at honours-degree level and the remainder at ordinary-degree or higher-certificate levels. Sure, the number of colleges in the CAO had increased, but only by a handful and not enough to warrant all the additional courses. Some Higher Education Institutions (HEIs) had between them ten to twenty different specialized courses within the arts, business or engineering. A number of these had only a small number of places to offer – as few as ten in some cases – which often resulted in them requiring higher points. Higher points suggested to parents and students that it must be a good course, so it tended to attract more of the limited pool of very bright students for which every institution was competing.

Ruairi was determined to add the points system to the ever-expanding list of items on his reform agenda. There was no great political pressure on him from Leinster House to do so. College entry doesn't feature highly in constituency clinics. Politicians long ago discovered that there is little or no point in making representations to the CAO on behalf of some constituent's son or daughter. It's the computer in the CAO offices in Galway that spills out the offers in a clinical and efficient manner, and it is one of the few areas of Irish life where 'pull' doesn't count for anything. But tackling the points system was a popular thing to do with parents, and it gained Ruairi huge kudos from the media, who make substantial revenues from ads in CAO supplements every year.

Fortunately, the National Council for Curriculum and Assessment and the Higher Education Authority had the same concerns and were jointly planning a conference in UCD a few months later, in September, by which stage Ruairi would be well into his brief. The conference was prompted by concern about the growing 'backwash' effects the points system was having on the Leaving Certificate – in other words, it was having an impact on the subjects students were taking and how they were studying. But who could criticize students for narrowing their focus to concentrate on getting maximum points to the growing exclusion of everything that couldn't be measured and scored?

Over the decades, students had learned to 'game' the system and were choosing subjects where they believed high points were easier to obtain. Geography and biology were cases in point. Agricultural science had recorded a 42 per cent increase between 2008 and 2011. There was evidence that agricultural science had become particularly fashionable among students in southside fee-paying schools in Dublin, which gave rise to jokes about them driving to school in their Ranelagh tractors. Other subjects, such as higher-level maths, were seen as harder. This prompted former minister Mary Coughlan to introduce a 25 per cent bonus in the points for maths for those who took it at higher level, a decision that has proven to be correct. In 2014, 27 per cent of all Leaving Certificate students took higher-level maths in the exam, compared with 16 per cent in 2011.

It wasn't just the gaming of the system and the selection of subjects that were of concern, but also what students were learning and how well they were being prepared for further study in higher education or indeed the world beyond the school walls.

Speaking to guidance counsellors in August 2010, Professor Tom Collins, then acting president of NUI Maynooth and chair of the National Council for Curriculum and Assessment (NCCA), was particularly critical of the points system, stating:

> There is growing anecdotal evidence that the system is no longer fit for purpose at third level either. There is a palpable concern in higher education regarding the capabilities and dispositions of students entering it straight from second level. The manner in which the points system rewards rote learning, instrumental learning and memorization, while simultaneously discouraging exploration, self-directed learning and critical thinking, means that even relatively high-achieving second-level students can struggle on entering third level.

And in an article in the *Irish Times* in May 2011, the former president of DCU, Ferdinand von Prondzynski, put it bluntly:

> Here's the situation. We have a final secondary-school examination that we all know isn't fit for purpose. It encourages learning methods that offend the most basic principles of pedagogy. Its curriculum is outdated and hard to change to something better. By all accounts it fails to engage the interest and enthusiasm of either teachers or students. It doesn't attract any respect from the wider world, including the world of business. It has little impact internationally.

The previous year, in February 2010, comments by the former Intel CEO Craig Barrett had startled both policy-makers and the public. In an interview on RTÉ radio he said Ireland would end up an economic backwater if it did not radically reform its education system: 'If you assume maths and sciences are key capabilities for the future . . . and you are not doing a good job educating young people in maths and science, you have a problem. That is why I told your government leaders you are coasting. You are living off what you did twenty years ago.'

His criticisms were seen as a wake-up call for education policy-makers. To some extent, his view that Ireland had become smug and complacent about its education system was correct. The IDA ad that greeted you when you disembarked at Dublin airport, with its background of bright young graduates and the message 'The young Europeans. Hire them before they hire you' fed into an unmerited sense of educational superiority.

Another wake-up call had been the 2009 OECD report from PISA – the Programme for International Student Assessment – which indicated a marked deterioration in Irish fifteen-year-olds' reading standards, below-average results in maths and just-above-average results in science. The PISA 2009 report was released late in 2010. The online publication *Education Matters* commented that the disappointing results of the PISA 2009 study were like 'salt on the wounds of an already smarting nation'. The poor results had indeed captured the downward spirit of the age, as people's confidence was eroding with the realization that the boom was over.

Barrett had argued that the Irish education system needed to be more competitive and that it should teach its students to be entrepreneurial. He criticized teaching by rote and rote learning and stated that the system needed to place more emphasis on skills such as innovation and critical thinking.

In this respect too, Barrett's was not a lone voice. The National Strategy for Higher Education to 2030, published in January 2011, reiterated the concern that second-level education did not prepare students adequately for the challenges of third level. It claimed that students entering colleges and universities directly from school often lacked the critical thinking, problem-solving and independent-learning skills required for successful engagement at that level. It pointed out that particular concern had been expressed about students entering higher education without the necessary skills and knowledge to engage effectively with learning in the disciplines of science, technology, engineering and maths (STEM).

The American Chamber of Commerce said that the points system should be reviewed and remodelled to reward creativity. It suggested that more points should be given for problem-solving-orientated questions and suggested that a specific problem-solving paper could be taken to supplement points.

So there was no shortage of concern from the experts and from industry, which the politicians also spotted. Ministers and education spokespersons joined in the clamour for change to make higher education more 'relevant' to the world of work, but they weren't as concerned about the need to change the points system. It just wasn't on their radar that much. However, it was on the to-do list for people in education and now for the new minister. But we had been here before, when Micheál Martin set up the Points Commission in 1997 under UCC's professor of education Áine Hyland (who was, incidentally, my supervisor when I did a master's in education). A rising young civil servant, Seán Ó Foghlú, was appointed to the commission, and was the driving force behind the publication of its background paper and the research papers. There was some minor tweaking after the commission's report, but no substantive change was recommended.

The problem was that, despite all the complaints about the points system, nobody could come up with a better one. Even if it were logistically possible, for instance, could you really have a fair system of interviews in a small country where influence still counted for so much? Or personal statements, for that matter?

But Áine Hyland and others were increasingly worried over the gaming of the system by students and the exponential growth in CAO courses, and they now had a minister who shared their concerns. In his remarks to the September 2011 conference, Ruairi called for a public debate on the issues raised. He quoted approvingly a comment made by the Irish Second-level Students' Union (ISSU) – 'The points race puts our young people to the pin of their collar physically, mentally and emotionally' – and asked what could be done to change it.

The debate had started, but it took a long time for the talk to translate into firm proposals. The teachers' unions, managers and principals were keeping a close eye on developments, as any changes would impact directly on their members. The unions were wary that proposals would emerge that would entail changes in the Leaving Certificate similar to those Ruairi was trying to push through at Junior Certificate level, which they rejected. But they really did not play any serious part in the discussions. By the following June, we were getting impatient with the slow pace and we put a critical line into a speech Ruairi was about to deliver to the university presidents.

Ruairi told them that they were the controllers of entry into higher education. 'Not me, not my department. Your decisions have a profound backwash effect on what happens in second-level schools and what subjects students choose for their Leaving Certificate.' Then he attacked them for their tardiness, saying that 'For the past few months I have been told regularly that a report from the university sector on what changes are planned is imminent. There is still no sign of it and I have to express my disappointment at the delay by the university sector in coming forward with concrete plans for change.'

He told them that they had a responsibility to broaden entry routes into undergraduate degrees so as to provide clarity of choice. This would reduce artificial point inflation and end the current needless subdivision of programmes. 'This issue must be dealt with first before we begin to look at the grade banding issues in the Leaving Certificate,' he added.

We deliberately leaked his comments to the education correspondents, much to the chagrin of the Irish Universities Association and the disapproval of some senior officials in the department. But Ruairi and his team felt it was time to put a bit of pressure on; otherwise, some other minister would still be pushing the same issue in five years' time.

But things were beginning to move. A task force was set up by the Irish Universities Association and chaired by Philip Nolan, president of NUI Maynooth. In an *Irish Times* interview with Joe Humphreys later, he said, 'All of us have become embroiled in a system where we've been using the points system to try to attract students in.' He said there were 'too many courses with very small numbers that are there for historic reasons to do with ensuring that points were not seen to sink too low . . . We need to get away from this sense that points are related to quality. Points are related to nothing but demand and supply, and it's a real shame if institutions, including my own, feel they should reduce the supply to make the points higher in order that it looks like the course is better; the course is no different.'

But he succeeded in getting the universities to agree to a major reduction in the number of separate entry routes to their courses, so that students would only have to choose between broad areas of study on their CAO form (arts, science, engineering, business, and so on). The actual details have yet to be worked out, but it was certainly firm movement.

In TCD, the provost Paddy Prendergast and senior lecturer Patrick Geoghegan began to get some movement on a reduction in the number of courses – not as many as we would have liked, but progress nonetheless. Trinity also introduced a pilot project under which a small number of pupils would be admitted on the basis of Leaving Cert results along with an anonymous personal statement of interest and their Relative Performance Rank (RPR) – a measure of their results against others in their school. It was an interesting experiment, but how it could be scaled up remains to be seen.

Coming into the summer of 2014, UCD deputy president Mark Rogers said: 'In the past three years, UCD has reduced its CAO routes for school leavers from fifty-six to forty-five, and I believe this could be further reduced. By broadening the entry routes and reducing the number of CAO codes, we are being fairer to a wider number of students.

There were other parts of the transition-from-school-to-college jigsaw, and it was time to put them all on the one board. Given his past experience with the Points Commission back in the late nineties, it was no surprise that Brigid McManus's successor as secretary general, Seán Ó Foghlú, decided to chair a Transition Reform group comprising representatives of the department, the universities, institutes of technology, the Higher Education Authority, State Examinations Commission and the National Council for Curriculum and Assessment. One or other of the advisers always attended the meetings, as did Áine Hyland, by now emeritus professor of education at UCC.

The Exams Commission was scrutinizing the question of inappropriate predictability in the Leaving Certificate, amid concerns that it was encouraging rote learning. We were also looking at reducing the number of grades in the Leaving Cert. Was it really necessary to subdivide B grades, for instance, into B1, B2 and B3? There were in all fourteen different grades, which was now seen as too many. We arranged to announce details about our proposals to reduce the number of Leaving Cert bands on Easter Monday 2014, but Niall Murray nearly scuppered our plans when he got hold of some of the details and published them in the *Examiner* in advance. As a poacher-turned-gamekeeper, I was both annoyed and bemused. Fortunately, it did not take off as a story until we released it the following Monday, when it got plenty of airtime and was the lead story in the morning papers.

Forty months after Ruairi came into office, the number of CAO course choices had actually gone up instead of down. But the public is now aware that there are too many of them for students to make informed choices and there is a commitment to reduce the number significantly. Ruairi's successor, Jan O'Sullivan, is due to get the report of the Transition Reform group before the end of 2014. Her response to it and subsequent action by the key players will determine how easily or otherwise Leaving Certificate students make the transition to college in the future.

10. The St Valentine's Day Massacre

If tuition fees were a touchstone issue for the Labour Party, the idea of a capital-assets test to help determine who gets student maintenance grants was anathema to Fine Gael. Higher-education grants were awarded solely on the basis of income. Earn below a certain income and your child qualified for a grant. Earn above, and they didn't. Ruairí wanted to change that system, which was open to abuse, and provision for the introduction of a capital-assets test was tucked away in the education budget estimates approved by the Cabinet in late 2011. It was intended that from September 2013 onwards the families of new college entrants would have certain capital assets as well as income taken into account. When it came to applying for grants, this would of course hit some farmers, businesspeople and professionals who were asset rich but income poor, at least in the year of application. The measure slipped under the radar of the Taoiseach's advisers and, as far as we were concerned, by the time they copped on and, inevitably, wanted it taken out, it would be too late. With a Cabinet decision under Ruairí's belt, all that was left for us to do was to work out with officials the details of how it would operate in practice. That's when it got tricky.

It took a few weeks after the budget was presented for the balloon to go up in farming circles. Both the Irish Farmers' Association (IFA) and Irish Creamery Milk Suppliers Association (ICMSA) sought 'urgent' meetings with the minister to discuss their concerns about the planned measure. As the rival organizations would not have welcomed a joint meeting, two meetings were slotted into the minister's diary on the same day in May 2012, but with a decent interval between them. The IFA turned up in Leinster House first and made the predictable noises. They were to be followed a short time later by the ICMSA. However, someone phoned our office to explain that the ICMSA needed to cancel because a named member of the association's delegation had to deal with an urgent personal matter. The higher-education officials who had been waiting for the meeting left Leinster House to go back to their offices. And then the ICMSA delegation showed up, fully expecting to sit down with the minister and officials. The call had been bogus – some unknown dirty-tricks brigade was at work to upset them. Urgent phone calls were made and the officials returned. Naturally, we never did find out who had made that phone call.

As the summer wore on, the issue of capital assets filled a gap in the so-called 'silly season' when not much is happening around the political system. That's the time of year when the Leaving Cert/CAO stories start to fill the pages again, so deputy political editor Michael Brennan picked the right moment to return to the capital-assets theme in the *Indo*. He talked up the threat to farm assets in one story and in another wrote that the department was also considering taking second homes and cash amounts into consideration. The *Sunday Times* followed suit, with the disclosure of a case where a farming family succeeded in getting a grant for their offspring, despite having more than €300,000 in the bank. Copies of the documentation had been leaked to us by an official who was enraged over the ease with which some people could still get grants. We passed on the details to the paper.

There was still a widespread view that farmers and the

self-employed were able to manipulate their income to invest in new machinery or offices in the year before their children were heading to college so that they would come within the threshold for a grant. This had been highlighted in the early nineties, in a landmark report usually referred to as the De Buitléir report, after its main author, economist Dónal de Buitléir. The report said bluntly, 'The means test is defective in that it fails to take full account of ability to pay – particularly since it ignores the accumulated wealth of individuals. Some people with clearly expensive lifestyles obtain grants, while others, who are very hard pressed, lose out.' At that time, it was found that one applicant's father had net assets of IR£500,000 but his 'reckonable income' for grants purposes was just IR£6,228. Another farmer had 122 acres and net assets of IR£215,000, but his annual income for grant purposes was only £15,000. It recommended that a capital-assets test be introduced. Predictably, that part of the De Buitléir report was shelved, but the issue never really disappeared from view. What was surprising to me, at least, was the work done on a possible assets test by officials. This work was continuing even while Mary Coughlan was Minister for Education, and everybody knew how sensitive she was to the views of the farming lobby, as she had made her mark nationally as a Minister for Agriculture.

The rules had tightened up since the days of the De Buitléir report, and it was no longer quite as easy to manipulate the system. In its intense lobbying campaign of the various political parties, the IFA went so far as to suggest that the current method of assessment of farm income for the maintenance grant actually discriminated against farmers by disallowing a number of expenses such as capital allowances, lease payments, stock relief and interest payments on borrowing for capital purposes. It insisted that farming was a low-income occupation, averaging €18,000 in 2010, as official Teagasc figures showed, and said that many farm families could not afford to send their children to college without a maintenance grant. If an assets test were introduced that included farmland, this, the IFA argued, would deny access to higher education for many young people from low-income farm families.

However, the fact that assets were still not taken into account clearly rankled with many in the Labour Party. In opposition, Joan Burton regularly tabled Dáil questions seeking information on the socioeconomic background of grant recipients. It was not readily forthcoming, as the information had to be compiled from sixty-six different awarding bodies. But when it was produced, it showed that a fair percentage of farmers' and professionals' children qualified for grants. Farming organizations argued that this reflected poor incomes and also the desire of farming families to ensure that their children, especially those who would not inherit the land, would get a good third-level education. The Labour Party was not impressed. The impression remained that many farmers and vintners could access grants for their children, while farm labourers and bar staff often found themselves marginally above the income thresholds.

Agriculture minister Simon Coveney made abundantly clear his opposition to farming assets being counted in the assessment of student maintenance grants when Ruairi and I met him and his adviser Aine Kilroy in early 2012. But he was equally clear that the place to take a decision was at the Cabinet table, and he had no problem with Ruairi tabling such a proposal. Others had, and it was becoming clear this was going to be a ding-dong between the two parties. 'I want blue blood on the street over this – ten thousand farmers outside the department protesting would be good,' a senior Labour aide said to me. But it turned out to be red blood instead. We had been trying for months to get a memo on the Cabinet agenda and Ruairí was getting impatient. He wanted to fulfil his promise – made in the winter of 2011 – to get back to the Cabinet with details of how an assets test would operate, but the Taoiseach's advisers continued to hold up the memo, pending further discussion. This was not too unusual, but the long delay was. All through 2012, the Tánaiste's people wanted to push ahead, even if it meant the inevitable row. There was endless to-ing and fro-ing at adviser and official level, to little avail, and finally we were called to a meeting in the Taoiseach's department on 14 February 2013.

The background mood music to the meeting was anything but helpful. Michael Brennan in the *Indo* had again ratcheted up tensions with a story about a Fine Gael backbench revolt over capital assets. The farming community was already nervous enough over the unfolding horsemeat scandal (when products from Irish beef processors were taken off the Irish and UK supermarket shelves because they contained horsemeat). The processors pointed the finger at Polish suppliers, but that didn't seem to be cutting much ice with the media or the public. On top of this, the government in general and the Taoiseach in particular were in trouble over a very inadequate response to Senator Martin McAleese's report into the state's involvement in the operation of the religious-run Magdalene Laundries. The report found 'significant' state collusion in the admission of thousands of women into these institutions. In its haste to publish the report as soon as it got it, the government did not have time to consider it in detail and prepare a response. Big mistake. The Taoiseach, while professing sorrow at the abuses revealed, did not issue an immediate apology, prompting criticism from other members of the Dáil and the general public, but particularly from survivors who had been institutionalized in the laundries. (He made up for it two weeks later with an apology that was heartfelt and eloquent and well received by the survivors.)

Concern over capital assets had been raised by backbenchers at Fine Gael parliamentary party meetings. Against this background, it was always going to be a hard sell to get the assessment of capital assets over the line with the advisers, never mind getting it through the Cabinet. The meeting took place in the room at the end of the second-floor corridor known as the Taoiseach's Dining Room, a bright, airy room with a big round table that seats about a dozen people. It's mainly used for meetings, but it's also where a Taoiseach can have guests to a private lunch. The room was the scene of a number of bilateral meetings between Labour and Fine Gael advisers. On this occasion, the only thing on the menu was the Labour team: we walked into a well-orchestrated ambush.

We had assumed the meeting was to discuss and negotiate the details of the proposals. These had been worked out largely by an interdepartmental group (but not entirely agreed by them, as the agriculture representative just kept repeating their opposition to farm assets being taken into account). We were suggesting a cut-off point on assets above which everything else would be considered. We were willing to negotiate the cut-off point above our stated opening position. We never got a chance. The officials were packed off to a waiting room. One of them, Mary Doyle, who had previously worked in the Taoiseach's department and was now in our department, in charge of higher education, was not the least surprised. Inside the Taoiseach's Dining Room were his top advisers, Andrew McDowell, Mark Kennelly and Angela Flanagan, who were joined by Aine Kilroy from agriculture and Damien Garvey, adviser to Jimmy Deenihan, the Minister for Arts, Heritage and the Gaeltacht. Opposite them at the big table were Neil and I, and the Tánaiste's advisers Colm O'Reardon, who left after fifteen minutes, and Jean O'Mahony, who said little or nothing. Neil and I felt outnumbered and outgunned.

I fumbled the ball when asked by McDowell for openers why the proposal was being brought to the Cabinet at all and not in the context of a wider sustainability report on funding higher education. I had always assumed that any minister can bring any memo to the Cabinet that he or she wants, even if it is going to be shot down in flames. I learned that day that it is the Taoiseach's prerogative to refuse to take it. And his people made it clear that the assets memo would not be taken unless it formed part of a package of proposals dealing with higher-education funding, which they knew Labour was dragging its feet on. It went on from there, going from bad to worse. The Fine Gael team devoured us.

The meeting went on for two very heated hours but, ultimately, we reached an impasse. Fine Gael would not accept any version of the capital-assets test that included farming assets or, for that matter, business assets. Labour couldn't accept any version that didn't. Mark Kennelly said they didn't want a row over it. They would cooperate with us on primary-school patronage changes but Fine Gael ministers would vote against capital assets – it was a red-line issue for them. We left chastened and disappointed by what became known as the St Valentine's Day Massacre. We rang Ruairi, who was in Brussels. He was disappointed but blasé about any harm to his personal reputation as a result of what I saw as a very damaging setback. In fact, he and the Tánaiste's advisers wanted to continue pressing the case. At a subsequent Labour advisers' meeting I said that the party couldn't win on this issue. Colm O'Reardon told me not to be defeatist.

To Fine Gael's credit, there was no immediate leaking of the detail of the St Valentine's Day Massacre and no crowing about it. Four months later, however, on his first day as a junior agriculture minister, Fine Gael's Tom Hayes was interviewed on RTÉ's *News at One* and bluntly asserted that the capital-assets test had been 'dropped'. This earned him a very public rebuke in the media from Ruairi, who insisted the idea was still on the table. He pointed out that Tom couldn't be expected to be on top of the detail, since he had been a junior minister for just a day. But the reality was clear at that point – no capital-assets test would see the light of day under this government if it contained any proposal to take farm assets into account.

11. The ever-expanding elephant in the room

When Noel Dempsey was Minister for Education and Science from 2002 to 2004, a high-powered review team from the OECD came to Ireland to discuss funding of higher education in this country. They were in Leinster House meeting TDs and senators at an Oireachtas Committee on Education and Science. Afterwards, they insisted on having a photograph taken to mark their visit. Instead of the traditional 'Cheese', when they smiled into the camera they all shouted, 'Fees!'

The OECD team were not the only international experts telling us we needed to bring back tuition fees, a prospect that always worries parents and sets off political alarm bells. The officials of the EU–IMF–ECB 'troika' that arrived to run our economy in November 2010 also took a huge interest in fees. Their detailed level of interest in education was surprising to me when I was made aware of it. What they wanted to know in 2011 and later was not if tuition fees were coming back, but when.

Funding of higher education is a totemic issue for Labour. But it's also the party's elephant in the room, and it's getting bigger all the time. After entering government in March 2011, the party was never allowed to forget a pledge that Ruairí Quinn signed outside the gates of TCD in the run-up to the general election. Tuition fees had been abolished in the mid-nineties when Niamh Bhreathnach held the education portfolio. A charge was, however, allowed for items such as registration and exam fees. This charge – the annual student contribution fee or registration fee – kept creeping up, rising by a staggering 922 per cent between 1997 and 2011. Ruairi's pledge was not to increase it any further.

I remember the occasion well, having covered it as a story for the *Irish Independent*. At the time I wondered why he was doing it, considering that a few days earlier he seemed to be a bit wobbly on the issue, acknowledging the dire financial state the country was in and the funding problems hitting higher education. I assumed, rightly as it turned out, that the pledge was to do with Labour's drop in the polls at the time. As a former Minister for Finance, he led the Labour charge in highlighting the destruction of the economy by the banks, the regulators and the outgoing Fianna Fáil–Green Party government. He was particularly scathing about Fianna Fáil and noted that 'The presumption that FF must be involved, in the national interest, is just mind-boggling, and yet that is what is there.' But here he was, just days before a general election that was certain to oust Fianna Fáil from office, signing a pledge which was likely to come back to haunt him, if things were as bad as he said they were.

I learned later – once I was an 'insider' of sorts – that it was a panic measure by the Labour backroom strategists, who were alarmed at the change in the party's support from the giddy heights of the 'Gilmore for Taoiseach' bandwagon that had started two years before the election campaign to the non-stop slippage in the polls in the run-up to the election and the real prospect of a Fine Gael majority government. As part of a strategy to stem the bleeding, Ruairi was told to sign the pledge – something he had resisted agreeing to until that point. It had been so different months earlier, when the polls were suggesting Labour would get 33 per cent or even 35 per cent of the popular vote, while Fine Gael was predicted to get around 24 per cent. In the end, Labour got 19.5 per cent and Fine Gael 36 per cent.

In the budget for 2012, Ruairi agreed to an increase of €250 in the registration charge. It was unpopular with students but politically more palatable than raising class sizes in primary schools, an option that had been taken off the agenda. The increase was of no use to the higher-education institutions, as their core grants were reduced accordingly in the same budget. Some university heads wanted a public campaign on the issue of funding and a return of tuition fees, but decided to bide their time. As one insider put it, 'After a period of measured wailing we will look at the issue of fees again.'

The €250 rise infuriated students, who saw it as a broken promise. It was not quite on the same scale as the Lib Dem 'betrayal' of a pledge in the UK where fees were allowed to rise from £3,000 to £9,000, but it rankled. Ruairi's defence was that the country was facing a very difficult time, more difficult than anybody had anticipated or realized, and that it had lost its financial sovereignty. He pointed out that 44 per cent of students did not have to pay the charge anyway, as they qualified on family-income grounds for a waiver, but that cut little ice with the public.

The increase was nothing more than a stop-gap measure. I argued that what was needed was certainty on student charges or fees for the remainder of the coalition's term of office, to get the issue out of the political way. We discussed it with Ruairi on a number of further occasions, but with no conclusion. As advisers, we were not in agreement among ourselves at that stage. Neil saw huge political danger for

Labour, but I saw huge danger for the education system if the issue were not addressed. I raised it with the Tánaiste's advisers on a few occasions – again with no conclusion.

Ruairi then took many people by surprise on 3 February 2012 when he announced annual increases in the maximum student contribution up to 2015, by which time it would reach €3,000 a year. The day he made the announcement, I had travelled with him to Limerick, where he was to attend the inaugural address of the new president of Mary Immaculate College, Fr Michael Hayes, and also deliver a speech to journalism students in the University of Limerick at the request of a former colleague from my old *Indo* days, Tom Felle, director of a course in journalism and new media.

Ruairi stuck to the prepared text about the media I had written with advice from press ombudsman John Horgan – not something he always does with scripts – and then engaged in a question-and-answer session with the students. One of the questions was about fees. Ruairi wrote the next day that he had 'deliberately leaked out the probable increase in student fees to €3,000 by €250 increases over the next few years. It is banner headlines in the *Indo* today.' (His dramatic announcement was not in his circulated script, and it was fascinating to watch the journalists at work that day. Bear in mind, this was a talk, followed by a Q and A between the minister and journalism students, so there was every likelihood of a story. All the main papers and RTÉ were there for the session, but only Barry Duggan from the *Indo* asked afterwards if the fees announcement was new. I confirmed that it was, and he knew he had a great story. A young freelancer spotted it as well and gave it to one of the tabloids, and the *Examiner* picked it up also. No doubt there were recriminations in other newsrooms that missed the story despite being represented there.)

If anybody thought that announcing the annual increases up to 2015 would take funding off the agenda, they were mistaken. Mary Doyle feared the country was in trouble because of the projected expansion of student numbers if more funding was not forthcoming for the higher-education sector. There was no need to ask the obvious question about that growth – where would the money come from? The amount that could be raised by the institutions from philanthropists or commercial activities would never be enough. And if the state couldn't afford more funding, then the only other source was the students – either through significantly increased fees or a graduate pay-back scheme of some kind. Back to the elephant.

Three months later, both the Taoiseach's and the Tánaiste's advisers were irate over front-page stories reporting comments made by the urbane, lawyerly CEO of the Higher Education Authority (HEA), Tom Boland. The HEA had given a briefing to the education correspondents the previous day on future expansionist plans for the system. When it was over and they appeared to have wrapped up, the *Irish Times*'s Sean Flynn innocently asked how they were going to fund it all, and the CEO told them about a new study that was being undertaken on funding higher education. The study was news to Sean, and to Katherine Donnelly from the *Irish Independent*, and was all they needed to write up a story saying that fees were back on the agenda.

This particularly annoyed the inhabitants of Government Buildings, as a referendum on an EU fiscal treaty was coming up a week later. There had been a decision across government to hold off announcements of any bad news until after the referendum – 'Operation *Titanic*', one adviser dubbed it. 'Can you please ask Tom Boland to keep his mouth shut over the weekend, as we don't want anything to upset the referendum result,' was the polite request from Angela Flanagan on the Taoiseach's side of the house, while Labour's Colm O'Reardon's response was more direct. He slapped the *Irish Times* down on the table in his office and demanded to know, 'Has anybody cut the balls off Boland yet?'

While all of this was going on, Student Universal Support Ireland (SUSI), the new agency for dealing with applications and the awarding of higher-education grants, was becoming a problem. 'SUSI goes Wong' was the headline waiting to be written as the stories got worse during the following few months, with tales of documents being lost, applications turned down for spurious reasons, lengthy delays in processing applications and, even worse, in paying the grants. Some of the real hard-luck cases were where students had to drop out of college or go elsewhere. Fine Gael's Michael Ring, Mayo TD and Minister of State for Tourism and Sport, sent Ruairi a scathing and personal letter about the crisis. I wondered what Ring was thinking: it would have suited neither minister if the letter got out, and didn't he realize it could be released in a Freedom of Information request? The president of the Institute of Technology in Dundalk, Denis Cummins, went on *Morning Ireland* to talk about a student having to sleep in their car because their grant had not arrived and they could not afford accommodation. If you were of a curious disposition, you might ask how the student could afford a car, but that wasn't the point. The student was entitled to the grant payment in a timely fashion, as had been promised when SUSI was held up as a shining example of good public-service reform. Miriam Lord wrote a funny piece in her *Saturday Irish Times* column about the Taoiseach presenting an award to SUSI some months before its troubles began. The piece was headed 'If Enda knew SUSI like Ruairi knows SUSI'.

The minister had to look at the inevitable review into what went wrong in the first year, which was carried out by the management consultancy company Accenture. It highlighted delays in providing sufficient initial resourcing and staffing for SUSI, the lack of an early-warning system when things were going wrong, insufficient testing of the system in advance and inadequate communication about key dates, deadlines and documentation required by applicants. It set out proposals for a more streamlined process, which were implemented. Establishing SUSI was the right thing to do. Apart from being a more efficient way of handling applications and payments of grants, SUSI will save the taxpayers money in the future. After all, it was bringing together in one centre the work done by sixty-six different awarding bodies – local authorities and Vocational Education Committees (VECs). All of the necessary improvements were introduced and the system worked well in the second year. SUSI was a delayed success, I told one special advisers' meeting – however, success stories don't interest journalists as much as the disasters. I should know. It's the nature of journalism to highlight problems, rarely the successes. If SUSI had been a rip-roaring triumph from the beginning, with everybody getting their grants ahead of schedule, it would not have attracted much coverage. But that's life in the media.

Everything added to budget pressures and hastened the day when Labour would finally have to confront the financial sustainability of higher education. The colleges were rightly complaining that they were taking in increased student numbers at a time of reduced resources, and were warning that quality was at risk. There was some slippage in positioning on international league tables, but it wasn't too dramatic. The various tables rank universities using different criteria and, for all their faults, are important, particularly to presidents. All universities aspire to be 'world class' and most want to be in the top one hundred, or two hundred, or whatever. But to do that you need a good funding base.

The problems facing higher education were becoming more and more obvious. Visitors might admire the shiny new research buildings in our universities, but the reality is that the universities are starved of capital funds for badly needed refurbishment of old buildings and replacement of increasingly outdated equipment. Benefactors may donate money for new buildings, but not for that kind of work. The problem is exacerbated by the other demands on the department's capital budget, the priority being to provide sufficient physical spaces for the rapidly rising pupil numbers in primary and second-level schools. To make matters worse, some institutes of technology are stretched financially. And there is no sign of a let-up in the numbers applying for third-level education, which are growing at a steady pace. If anything, the return to economic growth is only adding to the pressure on the colleges, which are expected to turn out more and more graduates with the right skills. A report from SOLAS (the successor to the training body FÁS) published in January 2014 predicted that by 2020 almost half of all jobs (48 per cent) will be held by people with third-level qualifications or higher. Already, skills gaps are widening in some areas of the economy, which have to be filled by overseas graduates, and this is likely to continue.

Sure, some further savings can be made by eliminating

unnecessary duplication in areas such as engineering, nursing, teaching, and so on, but these are medium- to long-term gains, not quick money-savers. But unless the funding issue was tackled, some in the universities said the only option was to cap student numbers, which would cause a political storm and create well-founded fears of damaging growth to the economy. Something or someone clearly had to give, but what or who?

To mix metaphors, the elephant in the room was now on the table and wasn't happy about being ignored for so long. The Labour people did come around to accepting the issue could no longer be ignored, but had concerns about the timing of any specific proposal, whether it be a return to tuition fees, differentiated fees for different categories of discipline, a loans scheme, graduate tax, or whatever. Obviously, many in Labour would prefer greater state funding, but that might not be acceptable to Fine Gael. All the solutions have political and administrative risks.

It was hard enough for Ruairi Quinn to accept the need for an increase in the basic charges for registration, exam fees, and so on, but it would be much more difficult, politically and personally, to stomach a return to tuition fees, which had been abolished when he was Minister for Finance. In the mid-nineties, he and Tánaiste Dick Spring had agreed that a tax covenant scheme that existed at the time would be abolished and the savings used to increase the block grant given to the colleges to make up for their loss of revenue from their students' fees. The covenant scheme was introduced to help taxpayers save enough money to send their children to college, but it was open to abuse. For instance, university academics, who had a nice perk whereby they could send their children to college without having to pay fees, could also save tax on 5 per cent of their earnings by signing a covenant. Niamh Bhreathnach has always insisted that the abolition of tuition fees was the right thing to do. 'The gates had been opened. Numbers attending third level today confirm the success of this decision,' she wrote later. Many researchers would disagree with her. Asking a party that had plummeted in the opinion polls to accept that it had made a major mistake was a bit too much. The Higher Education Authority had done some work, but it was agreed by the department and the HEA that more needed to be done. Fine Gael had raised the promised study on funding which was in the Programme for Government when we met the Taoiseach's advisers on St Valentine's Day. We could not delay it any more. The department and the HEA wanted a cross-departmental committee to take one last look at this issue and spell out the stark options.

Politically, Ruairí's team felt that a cross-departmental group would be entirely unhelpful, and that a group of external experts could do the same work, while also bringing badly needed visibility and public understanding to the issue. Either way, much of this work had been done before, and setting up a new group was in part a way of postponing the hard decisions on funding. That said, the explosion in student numbers deserved another look, and concerns abroad over loans schemes, which once seemed such a simple answer, were growing. In the US, student debt had tripled in eight years to $1 trillion (one thousand billion). In the UK, the projections for its student-loans scheme had gone awry, leaving the higher-education system as badly underfunded as it had been before fees were increased. Lessons needed to be learned before we went down the same route.

As is often the case in these matters, the eventual decision

was a compromise between what the officials and the minister and advisers wanted. We would establish an expert group,
made up largely of external independent experts but also
including representatives of the Department of Education
and Skills, the Department of Public Expenditure and
Reform and the Higher Education Authority. The question
of who should chair this group was clearly important. The
view of Ruairi and his advisers was that we needed somebody with a high international profile who could lead the
public debate. We had in mind somebody of the standing of
former president Mary McAleese. Unfortunately, she wasn't
available, as she was completing her doctorate in theology in
Rome.

But a person who we discovered was available was Peter
Cassells, former head of the Irish Congress of Trade Unions.
He was familiar with the politics of higher education, as he
had done some consultancy work in the sector, and was currently executive director of the Edward M. Kennedy Institute
for conflict resolution, which is based in NUI Maynooth. He
would need all his skills to produce a report that will spark a
reasoned debate and decisions. The expert group he was
asked to head will look at the demand for higher education,
the benefits to the individual and society, income/expend-
iture trends, efficiencies, financial performance and, last,
but by no means least, long-term funding. It is expected to
present options on how to fund higher education to the minister sometime in 2015, which will then be considered by
government.

The timescale is important. The reality is that no decision
on fees, or loans, or graduate taxes, or any variation of them
will be taken by the current government. But the parties
to the government and the opposition will have to spell

out their thinking on this crucial issue before the next election. The higher-education institutions will be hoping that the next government has sufficient gumption to take the hard decision early in its new term of office. Because, no matter what proposal or set of proposals the expert group comes up with, there will be an outcry, particularly if it means taking away free third-level education. As Enda Kenny has remarked from time to time, 'You can't take away from people what they already have.' For the Labour Party, the day may be fast approaching when it is finally time to bell the elephant.

12. Maximum plucking, minimum hissing

Most newly appointed ministers arrived at Marlborough Street fired up with ambitions to reform primary and/or secondary education but gave scant consideration to higher education. It's not for nothing the department was sometimes known as the Department of Schools and Teachers – a tag that many officials resented. The politicians' attitude was mistaken, and in an early memo to Ruairí I pointed out the dangers of not giving enough attention to higher education and the political risks in assuming it to be a trouble-free zone. I should have paid attention to my own memo: in due course I was to get a tough tutorial in higher-education realpolitik myself, at the hands of Brendan Howlin and Phil Hogan.

The legendary education minister Donogh O'Malley learned his higher-education lesson the hard way. O'Malley is rightly revered for the introduction of free secondary education in the late sixties. But what's often forgotten is that he also announced plans for an historic merger of Trinity and University College Dublin, an equally bold gesture. Had he not died so soon after his forty-seventh birthday, he almost certainly would have had to row back on his plan, as it could never have been implemented without the most God-awful succession of rows.

It took several years for 'the merger' to be decently buried. I remember it well, as it gave me one of my first major exclusive stories, shortly after I had gone into journalism from college. By the early seventies, the two university institutions had decided no merger could take place and had instead agreed a carve-up of disciplines such as pharmacy, dentistry, veterinary science, and so on, between them. A student contact slipped me a copy of the deal, and I got all the details into the final edition of the *Evening Herald*. They were repeated in the *Irish Independent* and the *Irish Times* the following day. A TCD spokesman was quoted as saying that TCD greeted the *Herald* story 'with an oriental stare', a neat academic way of saying he wouldn't confirm or deny it. But it was confirmed when the official document was released. That was that as far as the merger was concerned, most people assumed.

Donogh O'Malley was not the only one to discover that higher education was a fraught area. In the mid-seventies, the 'government of all talents', which included such intellectual luminaries as Conor Cruise O'Brien, Justin Keating and Garret FitzGerald, made absolutely no progress on the university question either. For all its intellectual firepower, the Fine Gael–Labour coalition got itself into terrible tangles when it decided to set up a Cabinet committee to 'sort out' higher education. Its 1974 plans for a comprehensive system of higher education became too controversial and never saw the legislative light of day. The plans were modified in 1976 and ditched entirely by Fianna Fáil after it returned to office in 1977.

Niamh Bhreathnach's Universities Bill setting out a unified legal framework for all the universities and a set of principles for higher education came within a whisker of an embarrassing Seanad defeat in the late nineties, mainly because the university heads had succeeded in raising the alarm about the perceived threat to their autonomy. The bill which she did manage to get into law took up an inordinate amount of time, and the list of amendments she had to table was much longer than the actual bill itself. She would have been better off politically, and from an historic point of view, if she had pushed through her Education Bill instead. It was her Fianna Fáil successor, Micheál Martin, who did and is credited with legislation that, for the first time, set out the rights and responsibilities of the main education players at primary and second level.

Shortly before Ruairí came into office, the fog over the higher-education scene lifted with the publication, in January 2011, of the Hunt report. A panel of experts, chaired by economist Colin Hunt, had been asked to examine Ireland's higher-education sector, and it came back with a twenty-year 'road map' for its future. The report pointed out that we had thirty-nine disparate higher-education institutions, but we didn't have a connected higher-education system. And a coherent system was what was needed to deal with coming demographic and economic shifts.

Once in office, we could see clearly the outline of the issues we would have to confront: first, the roles of the universities and institutes of technology, their links to each other and the related possibility of setting up technological universities. Second, there was the question of reducing the excessive number of teacher-training colleges. In short, we were talking about a radical transformation of the higher-education land-scape. Hunt was essentially offering a framework with a lot of detail to be filled in by the Higher Education Authority. But the devil is always in the detail, and that's where some of our problems started.

The HEA set about preparing plans to start putting flesh on the bones of some of the Hunt proposals. It sought external advice from an international panel. In the summer of 2012, I got wind of its contents. It included that old reliable – the merger between Trinity and UCD. When I alerted Ruairi that it was to be recommended by an international group appointed by the HEA, he hit the roof. 'Are they mad or what?' he said.

The idea had never quite gone away. At a superficial level, it had its attractions, and supporters such as Peter Sutherland, the former Attorney General, former EU competition commissioner and former director general of the World Trade Organization, and chair of Goldman Sachs International and the London School of Economics. He had canvassed the proposal from time to time. In an address to the Royal Irish Academy in January 2010, he suggested that the two should combine to create a world-class institution. 'We would have a top-twenty or even a top-ten player to compete in the big leagues and, if so, wouldn't that be the best thing for Ireland?' he asked, but nobody really seemed to take the idea seriously. (Of course, Sutherland's habit of pronouncing from a lofty height to his fellow countrymen and -women, particularly about higher education, probably made him a less than persuasive advocate of the plan. At a UCD dinner in November 2013 at which Ruairi and a number of us from the department were present, he attacked the 'dead hand' of the Department of Education and Skills. (When introduced to people afterwards, Mary Doyle would say, 'Would you like to shake my dead hand?')

The report commissioned by the HEA had been put together by a group of international experts and chaired by a Dutch academic. Such international groups are, of course, always expert, independent and objective. However, if carefully chosen, the members can read a 'steer' from whoever hires them about the desired recommended outcome of their report. The HEA was as capable as any of giving the right steer, so our suspicion was that somebody from the authority had suggested to the international team that a merger should be back on the table. It didn't matter who it was, because now the proverbial cat was among the pigeons.

There was never any question of suppressing the report, which would have leaked anyway or come into the public domain via the Freedom of Information Act. When a controversial report is published by a state body such as the HEA, the public is sometimes confused over whether or not it represents government policy. It may do, though it's also possible that it suits the government of the day to sit back and watch the fallout from a report, by way of testing the public mood on a particular issue. Of course, that's when ministers know the contents of such reports in advance. On the other hand, sometimes departments and ministers only become aware of the contents of reports very late in the day, and this can cause them a lot of headaches. And in a situation where a recalibration of the relationship between a state agency and a government department is already underway – such as was going on between the department and the HEA at this time – a contentious report can lead to an increase in tensions.

Sean Flynn of the *Irish Times* got wind of the controversial report. Although he didn't get his hands on the document, he knew enough detail to write a story on 25 September 2012 about the merger proposal. It inevitably caused ructions and, rather than try to delay publication of the report, leading to needless speculation, we realized it had to get out fairly quickly. We discussed what to do with the HEA. I remembered a phrase used by Mark Garrett from the Tánaiste's office when he described the timing of releasing reports as a form of 'traffic management'. And this incendiary report had to be managed well from our point of view. So when it was published in November 2012 we made sure that two others were published at the same time, late on a Friday afternoon when it was unlikely to get a huge amount of attention because of space restrictions in Saturday's or even Sunday's papers (most of the Sunday papers' pages being well mapped out by Friday evening, with limited space left for stories breaking on Saturday). The education correspondents were not best pleased to be landed with three reports so late on a Friday afternoon, but we wanted to bury the international report. As we had hoped, the Sundays did not bother running stories on the merger proposal.

Ruairi had to be careful not to condemn the report entirely out of hand, as it would not have looked well if one of the international experts appointed then went and resigned in protest. He had already responded to the early leaked version in September, along the lines that the merger recommendation was not in accordance with government or HEA policy and that it was 'neither feasible nor desirable'. He now added that, while the report contained very useful insights into the challenges facing higher education in Ireland, some of its recommendations were in conflict with already agreed policies and would not be acceptable to government. The merger story died again.

Much less attention was given to another recommendation in the international report for a national university of technology which would have various branches. This was a variant of the idea in the Hunt report suggesting that, where two or more current institutes of technology merged and where they satisfied certain criteria, they could become technological universities (TUs). Though it did not capture people's attention at the time, the ongoing issue of techno-logical universities was already fraught, and about to become more so.

The question of a university for the south-east was probably the most intractable problem in higher education. Waterford was one of the three areas looking for technological-university status. Its campaign was certainly the longest lasting. Back in the 1840s, at the time of the formation of the Queen's University of Ireland, local politicians had made strenuous but unsuccessful efforts to locate a university in their city. Instead, the three constituent colleges were set up in Belfast, Cork and Galway (the forerunners of QUB, UCC and NUIG).

In recent times, the focus had been on upgrading Water-ford's Institute of Technology (WIT). The city feels that inward investment is stymied by its lack of a university. The constant brain drain of very bright students to universities elsewhere affects the region in many ways, and local busi-nesspeople believe that it is difficult to persuade industry to invest in a region without a university.

The campaign was given a boost by a commitment in the coalition's Programme for Government to 'explore the establishment of a multi-campus technical university in the south-east'. This would come from the Waterford and Carlow Institutes of Technology combining to create a new technological university which would also have campuses in Wexford and Kilkenny.

In September 2011, after the announcement of the clos-ure of the TalkTalk call centre in Waterford with the loss of almost six hundred jobs, jobs minister Richard Bruton promised to fast-track the university, much to Ruairi's annoy-ance. There was no such plan, but whoever had prepared Bruton's briefing notes thought it sounded good and had not checked properly with us. The fast-track promise took flight locally, with Waterford Fine Gael deputy John Deasy heap-ing on the pressure. We had to prepare a briefing note for TDs and ministers explaining the correct situation, which did not please Bruton's adviser Ciarán Conlon, who asked me why the Waterford region could not get a university fast on the basis of regional needs. It was a bit more complicated than that, I explained.

We gave the correct timeline in terms of application and then preparation of a plan for technological-university status – assessment by an international panel, and eventual designation – to local TD, Labour's Ciara Conway, who spelled it out on Ian Noctor's WLR FM radio programme. The issue continued to bubble for a few days after Richard Bruton's initial comments. Ironically, it was his brother John who was Taoiseach when the Waterford Regional Technical College was upgraded to become an institute of technology. This re-designation of Waterford RTC – intended to boost its standing – was then demanded by all the other regional technical colleges in the country. This meant that the upgrade for Waterford conferred no real advantage over any other RTC and that it was little other than a name change. Ruairi's fear was that if a special deal were done to upgrade Water-ford further, to university status, without meeting agreed strict criteria, then other institutes would mount political campaigns to demand the same treatment, which would make a nonsense of the government's entire higher-education strategy.

The criteria for an institute of technology to become a

technological university are tricky to meet, as they relate to a certain threshold of students taking degrees at master's and doctorate levels, staff having Ph.D. qualifications, reaching a certain level of research activity, and so forth. Getting agreement on those criteria had proved extremely difficult because of the opposition of some university people and some board members on the Higher Education Authority, which was drawing them up. Some wanted to make the criteria so tough no institute would hope to reach them for over a decade. A number of university presidents took to ringing Ruairi directly to voice their fears about the whole system being undermined by the creation of technological universities with supposedly lower standards, which I thought a little OTT. There were echoes of the opposition to the upgrading of the Limerick and Dublin National Institutes of Higher Education to university status – when they became the University of Limerick and Dublin City University – in the late eighties (the latter referred to in political circles as 'Cape Canaveral', because so many launches of reports take place there). I told the HEA chair John Hennessy there was a political imperative in coming up with criteria that would 'stretch' the institutes, but not to breaking point. A compromise set of criteria was arrived at and published in February 2012. Some university heads saw them as driven more by regional and political needs than in order to meet rigorous academic criteria. They were described aptly by DCU president Brian MacCraith as the best that could be got, given the political circumstances.

I bumped into Carlow–Kilkenny TD and Kilkenny native Phil Hogan on the Ministers' Corridor one day, and he made it clear to me that he wanted university students in Kilkenny as part of the multi-campus university of the south-east spread across a number of locations, also encompassing Wexford, along with Waterford and Carlow. When I teased him that he already had two hundred students from NUI Maynooth on an outreach campus there, he joked, 'You can tell Maynooth to fuck off out of Kilkenny.' I also told him that the idea being floated by some in Carlow of locating the headquarters of the new university in Kilkenny seemed to me daft, as it would be hugely expensive to locate the central administration away from the two main campuses. A university president and his or her 'kitchen cabinet' of vice-presidents, registrar, and so on, should be on one campus. Even he didn't try to push that one.

Hogan has a touch of the hard man about him – the Fine Gael equivalent of the old-style Fianna Fáil bruiser and enforcer. He and Brendan Howlin, also a senior member of Cabinet as well as being a Wexford TD and Wexford native, held a meeting with Neil Ward and me about the government's commitment to a university in the south-east. We explained that there were difficulties getting the institutes of technology in Waterford and Carlow to progress their plans. Despite advance warnings from Neil that I shouldn't do it, I raised the possibility of Waterford linking up with the Cork IT. Neil had told me I would be kicked in the shins if I raised it. But I felt I had to, and had indicated to Ruairi that I would. He didn't demur, but didn't think I would get very far with it. The possible link-up was being canvassed by the Higher Education Authority, which argued that the strategic interest of the regions and the country would be better served by the creation of a single technological university embracing the existing institutes in Waterford, Cork, Carlow and Tralee. The HEA argued – persuasively, I thought – that combining all four would mean a clear potential for a multi-campus technological university of scale. With approximately 23,000 students, current income of over €220 million, 2,500 academic, support and research staff, and research income of €37 million, such an institution would offer enhanced benefits to students, enterprise and communities in the south and south-east, and it would have greater potential to compete internationally. The arguments had educational merit but were politically inconvenient.

Neil's warning had been well founded. Neither Hogan nor Howlin was having any of it, because they believed that Cork rather than the south-east would ultimately benefit from such an institution. While Howlin is usually fairly chirpy, I had seen him be very tough and angry. On this occasion, he was pretty uncompromising and far from chirpy. He was particularly irate when I suggested that the south-east could be beaten to the punch by Dublin, which was also looking for technological-university status. The two ministers threatened to bring their own proposals for a university in the south-east to the Cabinet if we could not make progress on the issue. I knew this prospect would alarm Ruairí, as it would inevitably spark off campaigns elsewhere for bypassing agreed criteria and procedures and demanding upgrade to university status. But as far as Hogan and Howlin were concerned, the promise was in the Programme for Government and that was it.

At the meeting, the ministers suggested that what was needed in the south-east was somebody to move things on. It took some time to agree on who that person should be. At Howlin's suggestion, Colin Browne, a senior Microsoft executive, was drafted in in mid-June 2013 to help knock heads together. A graduate of both WIT and IT Carlow, Browne seemed the ideal person, as his strengths lay in strategic management and enabling change. We hoped that his involvement would be the game-changer that was needed.

I got Phil Hogan to ring the presidents and chairs of both institutes to tell them what the government wanted.

Just before Browne was appointed, Sean Flynn had got wind of the difficulties being encountered between WIT and IT Carlow, and I arranged to meet him for an off-the-record briefing over lunch. Sean was also aware of the suggestion that the Waterford and Cork institutes should instead get together, the move favoured by the HEA. I was fairly frank with him, as I felt a bit of publicity might be no harm in jogging things along. (Sadly, he never got to write the story. Seconds after I left him in the downstairs bar in the Westin Hotel on Westmoreland Street, he collapsed and was rushed to hospital. He joked afterwards that I had spiked his food and then left him with the bill. But the collapse turned out to have been caused by a cancerous brain tumour that tragically killed him the following February.)

Following Browne's arrival, talks between Waterford and Carlow, which had been progressing at a snail's pace, began in earnest. But this was hardly a marriage made in heaven, as, for various reasons, the administrations at the two institutes had a history of mutual antagonism. It was aptly described by the maverick commentators in the online Network for Irish Educational Standards as a shotgun marriage.

Colin Browne soon discovered that academic politics are labyrinthine and that it is easy to mistake process for progress. I assisted as much as I could, but for a marriage to work you need two very willing partners, and I could only do so much. And after a few months Browne realized that, despite plenty of talk, little headway was really being made by WIT president Ruaidhrí Neavyn and chair Donie Ormonde and ITC president Dr Patricia Mulcahy and chair John Moore. (Neavyn was actually Mulcahy's predecessor in

Carlow. Waterford had assumed that appointing him as its president was a masterstroke and guaranteed to move things along quickly. But it did no such thing.)

Meanwhile, the south-east was not the only area looking for TU designation. The Dublin Institute of Technology (DIT) was determined to get university status this time after a previous attempt was blocked. It had opened up talks with the institutes in Tallaght and Blanchardstown. Ruairi appointed Professor Tom Collins, former acting president of NUI Maynooth and former president of the Dundalk IT, to chair the Blanchardstown governing body. Ruairi later appointed him to chair the DIT governing body too, a shrewd move, as it helped speed up the preparations for merging the three institutes. Dublin left nothing to chance, and the three ITs brought on board the former chairman of the Higher Education Authority Michael Kelly as an adviser. Kelly knew his way around, hence his wry comment, as he and his colleagues were confronted with Mary Doyle, her officials and me when they came into the department for a meeting, that they were 'glad to have a face to face with key decision-makers'. Still, he knew how the process worked, and that meeting was of some use in moving things along.

In the south-west, Cork, Tralee and Limerick institutes also lodged an application, but Limerick later withdrew, leaving Cork and Tralee to draw up a joint plan.

In the summer of 2014, detailed plans to get to the next stage of the technological-university process were submitted to the HEA by two of the three applicants – the Dublin alliance of DIT, IT Tallaght and IT Blanchardstown and the south-west alliance of Cork IT and IT Tralee. In September, an international team basically approved the plans with some modifications. Meanwhile Waterford and Carlow ITs effectively stood down Colin Browne because they wouldn't accept his approach, much to the annoyance of Minister Howlin, who balled them out and warned them it was their last chance to get a university.

The other key area on which both the HEA and ourselves were keen to move was teacher training. At first glance, this may not seem important to the general public. But if our primary and second-level teachers are not prepared properly, how can they be expected to be the best professionals they can become? The multiplicity of teacher-education courses and the huge number of taxpayer-funded institutions – nineteen in all – always bothered me, and early on I gave Ruairi a list of them. After all, these made up half of the higher-level institutions in the country (though obviously not catering for 50 per cent of the third-level-student population). He agreed it was too many. Fortunately, MAC member Dr Alan Wall, a senior civil servant, and the chief inspector in the department, Dr Harold Hislop, were also concerned about the need to improve teacher preparation. An international panel, headed by renowned Finnish educationist Pasi Sahlberg, produced a report in July 2012 which recommended that the number of providers be reduced to six and suggested that the centres should be based in universities.

Given that four of the five primary-teacher training colleges were Roman Catholic, the question arose about what to do with the Church of Ireland College of Education (CICE) in Rathmines, a venerable institution but expensive to run. Though saving money was not the main motivation behind the proposed rationalization – an improved quality of preparation in a university environment was – it was the case that the cost per student at CICE was considerably higher than in the four other colleges, so in its case integration into a larger college would save money.

The Sahlberg report was agnostic about which university CICE would end up with, but it became increasingly obvious that it would not remain within the embrace of TCD because relations between the college and Trinity's education department were deteriorating by the day. If you think national politics are tough, they are often not a patch on academic politics. The language may not be as crude, but the arguments are more pointed and better expressed. The very bitter disagreements were driven partly by personality clashes but were also due to the continued ethos of the CICE, whose students used to attend Trinity for a few hours of lectures a week and get their degrees from the university. The college claimed that Trinity was unwilling to allow for the retention of the CICE name or ethos, 'as the university and its school of education described themselves as strictly secular', a claim rejected by Trinity, which insisted it could continue to cater for a denominational college. Indeed, shortly after CICE broke off relations, Trinity did a deal with the Jesuits and opened the Loyola Institute, which is dedicated to teaching and research in theology in the Catholic tradition.

Anne Lodge, president of the college in Rathmines, had already opened up discussions with NUI Maynooth, where she had worked previously in its education department. But Ruairi and I had serious doubts about the political wisdom of the Church of Ireland teacher-training college linking up with Maynooth – try explaining to Northern unionists the difference between the lay-run National University of Ireland Maynooth and the co-located seminary called St Patrick's College, Maynooth. All they would see was Rome Rule.

I suggested to Anne Lodge that she meet with Daire

Keogh, president of St Patrick's College, Drumcondra. Ruairi thought it a great idea, although at all times he was clear that it was a matter for the Church of Ireland College itself. The outcome over a number of meetings was a decision by CICE to join St Patrick's and the Mater Dei Institute of Education (the Catholic post-primary teaching college) as part of a new DCU Institute of Education on an integrated campus in Drumcondra.

The decision was troubling in some ways, as many in the Church of Ireland were very unhappy with the move away from Trinity, even if the core curriculum of the new institute was to be non-denominational, while, to cater for the needs of both traditions, two centres of denominational education were to be established in the new set-up. But, crucially, the move had the support of the Archbishop of Dublin, Michael Jackson. To my knowledge, he attended more meetings on educational issues than any other bishop, Catholic or Protestant, in the forty months Ruairi Quinn was minister. The archbishop is known for his outspokenness about sectarianism and his masterly use of the English language. I recall one meeting in the department when we were discussing the likely reaction of the Church of Ireland to a particular education issue and he responded, 'The Protestant community might be described as particular, without being peculiar.'

Progress on the other proposals in the Sahlberg report was made in Limerick, Cork, Galway and Maynooth, where Froebel College was incorporated into the university and moved from Blackrock, County Dublin, to the university campus in Kildare.

Of course, local politics are never too far away when it comes to higher education. I had to brief Angela Flanagan from the Taoiseach's office about the report. She had a particular concern about the future of St Patrick's College, Thurles, where second-level teacher training was due to cease, an issue of concern to Fine Gael TD Noel Coonan in particular. In Sligo, Minister of State John Perry issued an optimistic statement about the future continuation of St Angela's College, over-interpreting a phone conversation he had had with Ruairi. This resulted in one of Ruairi's few moments of genuine anger, and he called John Perry again, reminding him very clearly that he was only a junior minister, and one with absolutely no influence over education policy.

Overall, the reshaping of the landscape meant a much deeper level of engagement between the department and the HEA than in the past, and it was throwing up questions about the future governance of the authority and its relationship to the department. The authority was the statutory planning and advisory body to the Minister for Education and Skills and a funnel for taxpayers' money to universities and other third-level colleges. It was one of a number of Education and Skills departmental agencies that enjoyed varying degrees of autonomy and importance. Other high-profile agencies included SOLAS, the State Examinations Commission, the National Council for Curriculum and Assessment and the National Council for Special Education. Lesser known but also worthy quangos were bodies such as the National Centre for Guidance in Education.

From 2012, it was an open secret in higher-education circles that relations between the department and the HEA were deteriorating. The rumpus caused by the UCD–TCD merger proposal was one reason. But there were also policy and personality differences between the no-nonsense Mary Doyle, who was in charge of the higher-education section in the department on the one hand, and HEA chief executive Tom Boland and chair John Hennessy on the other.

The very strong-willed Hennessy had worked with the Swedish company Ericsson, where he ended up as managing director of the company in Ireland. He took a hands-on approach to his HEA role and was certainly not one simply and passively to carry out government wishes. He wanted the universities, institutes of technology and other public-sector colleges to be more like the private sector and become more competitive. He said that there appeared to be limited effort to devise and implement a strategy to identify and reward institutions, faculties and individuals that were doing best. 'We must reward excellence and differentiate between institutions in higher education. We must reward and reinforce the right behaviours and differentiate within the sector,' he suggested. CEO Boland was very much the sophisticated intermediary who realized that this would not necessarily play well with staff in the colleges or chime with government policy on pay.

Hennessy's thinking was in line with that in the UK. It speaks volumes that there the universities come not under the education ministry but under the remit of the Department of Business, Innovation and Skills. Successive UK ministers have pushed their universities more and more into the path of big business. This is understandable – higher education is a key driver of economic and social development. The growth of our third-level sector is one of the main reasons so much foreign direct investment makes its way to Irish shores (along with our low corporation-tax rate and the fact that we are an English-speaking nation). However, Ruairí was always aware of the danger of the state seeing higher education solely through the prism of economic development.

As time wore on, the department was taking on greater responsibility for policy formulation and developing the view that the HEA should be an executive agency and that the relationship between the two should be akin to that between the Department of Enterprise and the IDA, that is, it should be an instrument of government policy. This did not go down well with some in the HEA, who believed that the authority should be a strong buffer between the third-level institutions and the state and a public advocate for that sector.

Despite these tensions, there was progress towards increasing transparency and accountability. After a lot of to-ing and fro-ing with the department, the HEA published various documents which had a fair amount of jargon about performance management, 'compacts' and KPIs (Key Performance Indicators), which were all about making the institutions more accountable. The HEA's main achievement was the very detailed report on a new higher-education landscape it published in 2013, which aimed to make a coherent system out of thirty-nine separate third-level institutions through mergers, greater collaboration and regional clustering arrangements. Ruairi's term of office set the scene for what is likely to prove the biggest series of changes in higher education for decades. Whatever about private rows over aspects of policy and decisions, this happened without any major public rancour; the scene-setting was done with the higher-education equivalent of maximum plucking and minimum hissing.

13. Cheesed off with FÁS

The removal of the Anglo Irish Bank name from outside the bank's former headquarters on St Stephen's Green in April 2011 was an iconic moment. Passing drivers honked their car horns and pedestrians applauded the dismantling of one of the most notorious symbols of Ireland's boom and bust years. It made the evening TV bulletins. So we thought why not do the same to the FÁS sign on its Baggot Street offices, with Ruairi doing the removal honours?

Admittedly, FÁS was not in the same disastrous league as Anglo Irish, but it had come to represent a culture of spending taxpayers' money in a profligate way on expensive meals, concert tickets, entertainment, golf, and business-class and even much more expensive first-class airline trips.

Paul O'Toole, the organization's quietly efficient director general, wanted a more subdued burial for the training and employment authority. O'Toole had replaced Rody Molloy after he had famously gone on *RTÉ Today* with Pat Kenny in November 2008 to defend the indefensible. Molloy had converted his first-class return ticket to Japan to two business-class tickets for his wife and himself. Public anger was rising over the disclosure of flights and other examples of waste and high spending at senior levels in FÁS, revealed in great detail by Shane Ross and Nick Webb in the *Sunday Independent*. Molloy's was a car-crash interview, especially when he said, 'We broke no rules or regulations. At the time we were doing it, it was standard practice.' His actions may have been within FÁS rules, but his words jarred with the mood of the country, which was feeling the first chill winds of austerity. Molloy, who had been publicly defended by Taoiseach Brian Cowen, rapidly became the scapegoat for wasteful spending of taxpayers' money.

We spoke after his disastrous interview and I suggested he should announce immediately that he was going to hand back any extra money the flights had cost over and above the economy rate. 'But I've done nothing wrong,' he insisted, and he was legally correct in that. I told him he was not in a court of law but in the court of public opinion. 'I'd rather resign first,' he said. The next day, after negotiating a pension settlement, he was gone.

The package may have been generous, but his fall from grace came at a personal price, as he has an instantly recognizable face and, in the immediate aftermath of his resignation, it became emblematic of everything that had gone wrong in Ireland. Like many others who fell from grace during the recession – such as Sean FitzPatrick of Anglo Irish Bank and Michael Fingleton of Irish Nationwide – he and his family had to contend with photographers camped outside their home for days on end, armed with the inevitable cameras with long-range lenses. FitzPatrick was pictured laughing on a golf course, which seemed to convey an indifference to the suffering the collapse of Anglo Irish had inflicted on the Irish people. The photographers were trying to capture something similar with Molloy living it up on a fat public-sector pension. But attending a GAA match in Maynooth wasn't quite as damning as playing a round of golf in County Wicklow.

I had known Molloy, and other senior FÁS figures, well in my previous life as the *Irish Independent*'s education editor.

The newspaper and FÁS had worked together on the Science Challenge programme, which encouraged students to take up science and placed technicians and graduates in NASA-related companies in Florida. (Former president Mary McAleese's daughter Emma was one of the graduate interns.) The *Independent* was even more heavily involved with FÁS in the successful Opportunities exhibitions in Croke Park, which offered information about careers and educational openings to tens of thousands of visitors every year. The Opportunities event was usually officially opened by the then Taoiseach Bertie Ahern.

As the *Independent* was the media partner, I had a lot of dealings with FÁS staff, especially Rody Molloy and director of corporate affairs Greg Craig, who was a well-known spokesperson for the organization. Craig invited journalists, including myself, on a number of FÁS Jobs Ireland trips overseas, when the authority and employers were trying to bring the diaspora back home to fill vacancies at the height of the boom.

The campaign had the full backing of ministers, many of whom jumped on the Jobs Ireland and Science Challenge bandwagons and travelled abroad with FÁS (at FÁS's – or ultimately the public's – expense). When she was the enterprise, trade and employment minister, Mary Harney went to Florida with seven others on the government jet in July 2004 to visit the science programme. She later hit the headlines when it emerged that the $410 bill for her hair-dos was paid for with an FÁS platinum credit card.

Few questioned the massive amount of money the government was giving to FÁS at a time of very low unemployment. But the days of junkets and dinners at the taxpayers' expense came to an abrupt end with the onset and onslaught of the recession. Detailed audits were conducted and an investigation held after which disciplinary action was taken against a number of individuals.

Spending was one issue, but what was more damaging and what upset the staff in the organization even more were the serious questions being raised about the validity of certificates issued for some FÁS courses. The issuing of certificates had to be suspended for a time because of questions over how FÁS results were processed. To compound matters, a FÁS executive was arrested and later jailed for defrauding the organization of €600,000. It was the perfect media storm.

The first politician to call for the scrapping of FÁS was Ruairi Quinn, when he was in opposition. The decision to replace it was announced by Minister Mary Coughlan before she left office, but it would happen on Ruairi's watch. Ironically, he had been Minister for Labour two decades earlier, when the government had decided to set up FÁS, pulling together the old National Manpower Service, AnCO and the Youth Employment Agency.

FÁS had served as a Swiss Army knife for successive governments, with different parts of the organization and its 2,200 staff doing different things. It covered everything from apprenticeships – where FÁS had a good record of producing winners in the World Skills Competitions – to community employment schemes, Youthreach centres for 'at risk' teenagers, skills training, a vacancies service, careers advice and placement, research on labour-market and skills issues, travellers' centres, and so on. Coughlan decided that responsibility for policy and budgets in the employment and community-services areas was to transfer to the Department of Social

Protection, with about 40 per cent of staff and half its €1 billion budget. FÁS saw its future as a leaner skills agency, a proposal which certainly had merit.

But both parties in government wanted something new, rather than a FÁS Mark II or Continuity FÁS with just a name change. Radical change was needed. But what shape should it take? The Taoiseach's people had ideas, in particular Andrew McDowell. Some of their more extreme notions included privatization of training altogether, which would make a lot of FÁS trainers redundant, or the introduction of a voucher scheme or some other way of implementing the money-follows-the-client principle. Under the latter approach, jobseekers would be given some guidance but would have varying degrees of autonomy to pick and choose what they wanted to do, and the training would follow. With poker-faced Andrew McDowell, you never quite knew how much he believed in all of this nonsense, or if he was just testing how far he could push a 'small government' approach. I was involved in some of the discussions, with officials Dermot Mulligan and later Peter Baldwin leading on our side.

We had to produce arguments, citing international evidence, to push back some of the Fine Gael suggestions while at the same time clarifying our own thinking back in the department on how a new authority would operate. The idea of an unfettered voucher scheme where jobseekers could decide what they wanted to do has a superficial attraction. But at one session in Government Buildings I raised two questions: what happens if ten thousand people want to do courses to allow them to install water meters and the country only needs two hundred – what then? Second, what's to stop private providers of courses in popular areas such as computer skills advertising in the local media, talking up 'guaranteed' jobs in the IT sector for the 'right' people with the 'right' skills and enrolling tens of thousands of voucher-waving and desperate jobless? It might be small government, but it would be a big waste of public money and raise unrealistic expectations among jobseekers. The questions were left hanging.

Fortunately, there was a third way. Around this time, Ruairi was pressing ahead with plans, initiated by the previous government, to reduce the number of Vocational Education Committees. The VEC system had developed expertise in the further-education area, especially at post-Leaving Certificate course level. But there were too many committees, all with their CEOs, administrative and secretarial staff – thirty-three in all. Some were tiny, with only a handful of schools to look after, while others, like the City of Dublin VEC, had around two dozen centres to manage. The previous administration had announced its attention to reduce the number of VECs to sixteen, and the sector was already braced for the changes that were coming down the track. But now, with the break-up of FÁS, the changes were to be more far-reaching than they expected.

It made perfect sense to transfer the FÁS training centres to the smaller number of VECs. Though scepticism abounded within the different cultures of FÁS and the VECs, bringing them together was not as radical an idea as it seemed. Many European countries had developed a unified further-education and training sector over the decades which had high status and added high value. Ireland had gone a different route, with separate vocational education and training systems. It was time to end that and have a joined-up approach, particularly as there was some overlap between the activities of the two bodies. Not all the VECs were convinced. At a meeting in the Davenport Hotel organized by Michael Moriarty, general secretary of the Irish Vocational Education Association, Ruairi declared that their traditional turf wars with FÁS were over and the VECs had won. Many of the CEOs and representatives of the VECs present at the meeting didn't exactly look victorious, and it was clear that they didn't immediately recognize the opportunity they were being handed. Instead, they were still smarting over the reduction in the number of VECs.

Continuing to call the new sixteen committees VECs would be too limiting, so Ruairi decided on a new name, Education and Training Boards (ETBs). The name captured their roles entirely. As well as looking after local provision of education and training, the boards would also continue to run community colleges, Youthreach, outdoor-pursuits and other centres in the same way VECs had done for decades.

Next on the agenda was the crucial matter of how the new unified system would be funded, how it would be administered, how the provision of courses would be coordinated to avoid unnecessary duplication and to ensure gaps were plugged to meet local or national skills needs, how its activities would tie in with the activities of other departments, and so on. The obvious solution was a central coordinating unit that would proof plans for further-education and training provision from the new sixteen ETBs, audit and ensure the high quality of that provision, scale funding accordingly and tender for additional courses to plug gaps identified through research on skills requirements.

Several months of fighting with both the Taoiseach's and Tánaiste's advisers lay ahead before government approval was secured for the establishment of the new body. We had to talk Fine Gael out of some of their more extreme views, such as the introduction of a voucher scheme, while accepting that there would be increasing competition between providers of programmes, private and public. A significant percentage of courses under FÁS – at least 65 per cent – was already contracted out, and Fine Gael was anxious that this be stepped up. Minister of State for Training and Skills Ciarán Cannon was helpful in trying to move agreement forward with Fine Gael. Cannon didn't go along with some of the right-wing ideas of the party's ideologues, but never criticized them openly. He saw the potential of a high-class and high-status sector emerging which would prove to be attractive to young people who wanted to get real skills for life and for work.

Having squared off the Taoiseach's people, we were still encountering problems with the Labour side. The board of FÁS had been replaced in January 2010, and the new board, along with its director general Paul O'Toole, had done good work to improve its financial and management and other practices. Some members had an expectation that the board would remain in place when a successor body for FÁS was introduced. Both Colm O'Reardon and Jean O'Mahony were insisting that the board be replaced as well. I argued that this was unfair on the board members, who had done the modern-day equivalent of cleaning out the Augean Stables by bringing in lots of worthwhile reforms to the FÁS procedures. But I was in a minority, and the board was replaced – some were not best pleased that their services were being dispensed with, but the political system needed a clean slate. The final composition of any board is always fraught with possibilities for political rows, and the board of this new further-education and training agency was no different. Minister Joan Burton's special adviser, Ed Brophy, made it abundantly clear she would not be happy with having just one nominee on the board, as we were suggesting – she wanted four out of the thirteen places, but she compromised on it. In fact, the composition of the board was a compromise share-out between Fine Gael and Labour nominees, all of whom came through the Public Appointments Service. At least no one could say the new board members were in it for the money: previously, FÁS board members were given an annual allowance of €12,000 a year, but there was no remuneration for serving on this new board.

Thus a new unified system was finally agreed, but the question was what to call it. We couldn't simply name it the Further Education and Training Authority, FETA. I pointed out at one meeting in the department that the initials would be a gift that kept giving to sub-editors whenever a problem arose with the new body. The two obvious examples of the headlines they would come up with would be – trainees 'cheesed off' with FETA courses or 'something stinks' in FETA. We had to come up with something different and positive sounding. I suggested something in Irish and approached Muireann Ní Mhóráin, the head of the state body that assists with Irish-language material for schools, with a request for help, giving her the various words we would like translated. She came up with a few options, the best of which was the acronym SOLAS, which we liked immediately. The initials stand for An tSeirbhís Oideachais Leanúnaigh agus Scileanna, which is a reasonably good approximation of 'further education and training authority'. That the word *solas* is the Irish for 'light' was a happy coincidence.

While Ruairi liked the name, we knew it would upset some organizations, such as Waterford's Solas Centre, a terrific cancer-support group. It complained, as did a company with the same name which threatened legal action. We also had a few unexpected complaints from parents. Ruairi received a letter from a mother whose new daughter was baptized Solas. I phoned her to explain the reason for our choice. We also heard about another mother who has similarly baptized her daughter Solas but was now planning to change her new daughter's name by deed poll as a result of the new authority being set up. The domain name solas.ie was essential, but we discovered it was owned by TCD, which used it to provide a very useful health-information programme. We had no option but to put pressure on Trinity after our first approaches were gently rebuffed. Ruairi asked to meet the provost elect, Paddy Prendergast, in Buswells Hotel, where we explained our problem. He agreed to help transfer the domain name to the department. Once it did, SOLAS was formally established on 27 October 2013.

Bringing together two different cultures was always going to be difficult, but especially with two that operated in different time zones. FÁS centres had always operated on a twelve-month basis, and we had been quietly saying that further-education provision would have to change and do the same, as it's clearly unfair to tell a jobless person to wait until the further-education colleges reopen in September while training centres under the same ETB are still in operation. Ruairi raised the idea of year-round provision in further-education colleges at the Teachers' Union of Ireland congress at Easter 2014. Predictably, it led to a furious reaction from the union, providing a lead story for the *Irish Times*. The union's president, Gerry Craughwell, said that Ruairi Quinn had become the Minister for Announcements.

There was no suggestion that all further-education staff would have to work twelve months in the year, as some claimed, but what was made clear was that tutors and lecturers would have to be more flexible in their delivery of programmes. Ruairi couldn't very well state it, but to those who could read the tea leaves the message was that if the TUI leadership did not bring along its members on this issue, then other providers, particularly those in the private sector, would fill the gap, with the active encouragement of many in Fine Gael.

SOLAS, under its first CEO, Paul O'Toole, has produced a five-year strategic plan for the whole sector. The new body is now responsible for funding, planning and coordinating a wide range of training and further-education programmes. It's been instructed by government effectively to ensure the provision of high-quality programmes to jobseekers and other learners. It will also play a key role in updating the apprenticeship system, following a report drawn up by a committee headed by Kevin Duffy from the Labour Court. To borrow the phrase of the moment, the aim is to create a 'world-class' further-education and training sector. FÁS, the organization Ruairi was responsible for initiating twenty years earlier, had done the state much service for a long time but fell because of bad management and bad habits. SOLAS, the new organization he was now responsible for initiating, is determined to take on board the lessons from the past.

Ruairi never did get to remove the sign from its headquarters in Baggot Street. We discovered it was welded on tightly and wouldn't come down easily. The last public image of FÁS we wanted was a photograph of the Minister for Education and Skills up a ladder trying to remove a sign that wouldn't budge. By that stage, Ruairi was turned off by the idea anyway, so in July 2013 FÁS was allowed a quiet passing, well away from the public gaze.

14. Fee-paying schools under pressure

Fee-paying schools will always be a bugbear for the Labour Party and left-leaning organizations such as the unions. It's easy to see why. On the face of it, it is a simple story of elite schools with pampered pupils, small classes, great facilities and locations, often surrounded by rolling acres of fertile land. At least three fee-paying schools have golf courses. One is a nine-hole course on the 150-acre site of St Columba's College, a co-ed boarding school in the Church of Ireland tradition nestling in the foothills of the Dublin Mountains. Its Georgian and Victorian buildings are straight out of a Harry Potter movie. It has a warden rather than a principal, and if you have to enquire about the fees, you really can't afford them. Outside the capital, there is another nine-hole course at Roscrea College, a seven-day boys' boarding school, the only school in the world run by Cistercian (Trappist) monks, and the third is on the extensive grounds of the Jesuit-run Clongowes Wood, also a boys' boarding school. The website golfmaster.ie suggests that you don't bother putting it on your itinerary for a casual game if you are visiting County Kildare, as it is for the use of Clongowes Wood and Clane Golf Club members only. And once you leave such a school, lifelong inclusion in their powerful old-boy and old-girl networks ensures that you have access to people of influence to help smooth your path in life.

When newspapers publish tables of the fees charged by these schools – which can be eye-watering (close on €20,000 a year for some of the boarding schools) – and then also point out that they get almost €100 million from the state by way of payment of teachers' salaries, the reaction is predictable. Outrage. From an optics point of view, it is hard to justify the state 'subsidy' for these fifty-five schools when their disadvantaged counterparts are clearly suffering from cuts, or about to lose another teacher, or when parents of a child with special needs are having essential educational supports slowly whittled away.

It was obvious that fee-paying schools would be on the shopping list for the coalition's first budget in December. Changes in the pupil–teacher ratios at both primary and second level were on the department's list of possibilities from day one. They had to be, as the new government was looking to save a lot of money and teachers' jobs were a huge item of expenditure for the department. Fee-paying schools would not escape; the only question was how badly would they be hit. We were politically under a lot of Labour pressure to hit them really hard. Backbenchers such as Eamonn Maloney wanted the funding removed entirely from these schools. It seemed to me that Labour had not really thought through what 'hitting them hard' meant; nor did we know enough about the disposable income the fee-paying schools had. Hitting fee-paying schools for the sake of it would look almost vindictive to our new partners in government and would inevitably lead to a backlash from Fine Gael, particularly if it threatened the future of Protestant schools. I argued that we needed more information on the country's fifty-five fee-paying schools on which to base informed policy and decisions. The Labour Party policy, it seemed to me, was ill thought out, and some kind of review would provide political cover and buy us time while we worked out what exactly was to be our position on these schools.

What I had in mind was commissioning a report which would be undertaken perhaps by the Economic and Social Research Institute (ESRI). It had already been examined in a relatively recent government report, the McCarthy report into public spending in 2009, also known as the report of An Bord Snip Nua. It recommended a 25 per cent reduction in the state subvention in the first instance. This would be achieved by a significant worsening of the pupil–teacher ratio, which would result in a 21 per cent increase in fees. Ruairi liked the idea of a review. After discussions with officials in Dublin and the schools section in Athlone, we agreed that it would be undertaken internally under Martin Hanevy's direction. This gave us some cover, but fee-paying schools remained in the politicians' sights.

In the first Fine Gael–Labour budget, it was announced that the pupil–teacher ratio in fee-paying schools would rise to 21:1, and that the department would conduct an analysis of tuition-fee income available to these schools and the uses made of the extra revenue. Throughout 2012, tensions over fee-paying schools were rising, and the Tánaiste's advisers kept pushing fee-paying schools as an issue. The animosity towards the private schools was very evident at the Labour Party conference in Galway in April 2012, where delegates demanded an end to public funding of fee-paying schools. Such was the atmosphere, it would have been a brave or foolhardy individual who stood up to defend such schools or voted against the motion. Whatever his views, Ruairi had no option but to go along with it, even though he himself is a product of one such school (Blackrock College), as are other members of the Cabinet. The motion passed, and it remains part of Labour policy.

However, the picture on fee-paying schools was far less clear cut than either the dramatic newspaper features or the rhetoric of delegates at the Labour Party conference might allow. The reality was – though many in Labour didn't want to hear this – that abruptly withdrawing the entire state subsidy of €100 million from these schools, which served about 26,000 students, would lead to educational havoc. I believed the schools could take another hit, but not to the extent of entirely withdrawing state support. If that happened, some wealthy schools, such as St Columba's, would survive by jacking up their fees, and they would become even more elite. But many would have to close, forcing the state to provide places for students in often overcrowded schools in the free scheme. There would be little or no savings to the state, probably the reverse, as places would have to be provided for the students elsewhere. Others would try to join the free scheme, but I suspected (and the department subsequently discovered) that it would be an expensive and time-consuming exercise negotiating entry into it, because allowances have to be made for transitional arrangements, which would be costly.

Finally, withdrawing state support to fee-paying schools would have an enormous impact on Protestant schools outside Dublin. Some would have to close. This would have had serious ramifications for the state's relationship with the Protestant tradition and cause a huge backlash among Northern Protestants. For historic reasons, most of the Protestant schools remained fee-charging when Catholic schools had entered the free-education scheme back in the late sixties. When the then minister Batt O'Keeffe removed the Protestant secondary fee-paying schools' special grant in 2009, he was accused of sectarianism. A remarkable photograph appeared in the *Irish Times* of O'Keeffe meeting a delegation from the Royal Black Preceptory in Leinster House when they were complaining to him about discriminating against their Southern brethren. The Royal Black is mainly made up of senior members of the Orange Order, hardly a shining example of inclusivity or the best-placed organization to lecture a government in Dublin about treating minorities fairly.

Shortly after the Labour Party conference, I, with DES officials, met an alarmed delegation from a Protestant fee-paying secondary school. I had to reassure them that passing the motion at a Labour conference was not binding on the government as a whole. I could have added that the Fine Gael partners would not have allowed it to be implemented anyway.

In October 2012, junior minister Alan Kelly went further than we might have liked on *The Week in Politics* on RTÉ One by saying that worsening the pupil–teacher ratio was on the cards, rather than on the table for consideration, as he had been told by our press officer, Deirdre Grant. He had made it sound more certain than it really was at that stage. He said the days of the state giving a subvention to private schools were 'going to come to an end'. His comments provided a lead story for the *Irish Daily Mail*, and Christopher Woods, principal of Wesley College, went on *Morning Ireland* to express concern on behalf of the sector.

The Taoiseach's chief of staff, Mark Kennelly, had a pop at me over Kelly's remarks a few days later. I was meeting him to discuss, once again, board appointments, and he used the opportunity. I explained how it had occurred, but he wasn't happy about the impression created that a decision had been taken by the Cabinet when clearly it had not.

Later, Katherine Donnelly from the *Irish Independent* told me that she was aware of three Protestant secondary schools that were talking to the department about joining the free scheme. They were, but I could not confirm or deny anything. We had given the schools an absolute assurance of confidentiality. I had attended a meeting that very morning with one of the schools, and I had to ring one of those in attendance to reassure that person that, if any story were written, the details did not come from us.

Our budget discussions in the lead-up to December 2012 were taking place in a fraught atmosphere. In the background were clashes between the government parties over Labour's demand for a higher rate Universal Social Charge for those earning over €100,000. This was matched by Fine Gael saying it would only be done if Labour agreed to cuts in social-welfare payments, including the dole.

Matters were not helped by the leaking of a transcript of what Ruairi had said to the Parliamentary Labour Party about health minister James Reilly. In its lead story on 2 December the *Sunday Independent* reported that 'Ruairi Quinn, in a behind-closed-doors meeting, has said fears held by Labour backbenchers that Health Minister James Reilly is "not up to the job" are "shared by your Cabinet colleagues". Pleading with his colleagues that his comments "must not leak out of this room", he called on his colleagues "to be careful", saying the party "can't be seen to be looking for a head".' Incredibly, a thread on politics.ie suggested that Ruairi himself had leaked the story to the *Sindo*, which was nonsense. He made it clear to us the next day that he was annoyed over the leak.

I knew I would get the brunt of Fine Gael anger when I turned up for yet a further meeting about appointments to boards of various education bodies with Mark Kennelly in

Government Buildings the next day, forty-eight hours ahead of the budget. I was kept waiting in an office next door while he closed the door to his to make an 'urgent' phone call that lasted twenty minutes. When I was ushered into his office, he laid into me, demanding to know, 'When is your man going to apologize to Minister Reilly?' That was at lunchtime, and what surprised me was that nobody from the Tánaiste's side had sought to smooth things over by then, given the evident tensions and pre-budget nerves in both parties. My sense of Reilly's relationship with Labour people was that it was distant but cordial. He was one of those who always said hello but didn't give much away in chats with them.

When it came to the ostensible subject of the meeting – board appointments – Kennelly said that Labour had got more than its fair share of positions on education boards and 'We want ours.' Officials would have preferred it if appointments were strictly on the basis of suitability, but where board members were appointed by ministers, Fine Gael was more insistent than Labour on appointing 'its' people.

The conversation inevitably turned to the burning issue of fee-paying schools, which had recently been discussed in the Cabinet as part of the budget deliberations. What Ruairi had proposed to do was to worsen the pupil–teacher ratio over a three-year period in the fee-paying sector. This had been agreed by the Labour side but had run into heavy and predictable opposition from Fine Gael. After a small change in our first budget, the state paid the salaries of one teacher for every twenty-one pupils in these schools, compared with one teacher for every nineteen pupils in schools in the free-education scheme. The proposal was to raise the ratio to 24:1 in 2013, then to 27:1 the following year, and to 30:1 in 2014.

Ruairi argued that this was an equitable solution, which would give the fee-paying schools their sought-for certainty in the future, rather than having the annual uncertainty about what was coming in the next budget, which made planning impossible. They would then individually have to decide if they could survive on higher fees from parents or should join the free scheme. He acknowledged that he accepted the reality that a tiny number might even have to close.

Ruairi had used information from Martin Hanevy's analysis, which was now available internally, to bolster his case. The report, which we had for a few weeks, showed that the fifty-five fee-charging schools had a gross income of almost €117 million from fees, which ranged from €2,550 to €10,065 a year for day pupils. This amount reduced to €81 million when allowance was made for discounts on fees, unpaid fees, capital-loan repayments and estimates of forgone grants, including teacher salaries. In other words, the fee-paying schools had a lot of extra money to spend to privately recruit additional subject teachers and extra ancillary staff, or to invest in capital improvements and extra-curricular activities. The average discretionary income per fee-charging school was found to be €1.48 million. The amount varied considerably, with some large schools having more than €4 million extra a year to spend.

Kennelly made it clear he was not impressed by Hanevy's report, describing it as 'nasty'. Presumably it was nasty because it showed in black and white that the private schools had discretionary money of their own, which didn't suit the Fine Gael position that any reduction in state support would fundamentally undermine the sector. But Fine Gael ministers wouldn't accept Ruairi's proposal, and all they would agree to was a one-year worsening to 23:1. Kennelly had made it clear to me, 'But that's that. We won't wear another one.' And they didn't in subsequent budgetary discussions.

The twenty-minute delay – deliberate or otherwise – before I could see Kennelly that day had made me feel like a supplicant at the gate waiting to be ushered in to see one of my betters. It was the source of some mirth afterwards to the Tánaiste's advisers when I told them, one of them remarking, 'Ken Clarke was always pulling that one.' For me, it was another fascinating exercise of power.

We finally got to publish the fee-paying schools report in March, when it sparked off a major debate on the future of the sector. This was four months after we had received it. People might wonder why it was not published sooner, but it's not unusual for reports to take much longer to work their way through the system and be officially released. (And a few never see the light of day.) The report was a solid piece of work by Martin Hanevy and his team, even if part of it had to be rewritten to make it more reader friendly.

Hanevy is something of an old-fashioned fixer, and his ability to sort things out came in very useful when talks began in earnest with a number of fee-paying schools which were considering their options, including joining the free scheme. Both Neil and I got involved in many of the subsequent dis-cussions, which resulted in four schools joining the scheme, with others waiting in the wings to see how things played out. I attended one meeting with a fee-paying school which wasn't so much interested in joining the free scheme as get-ting the state to appoint half a dozen extra teachers so that it could become a centre of excellence. Touching, but naïve.

It wasn't just the worsening of the pupil–teacher ratio and the reduction in state support that prompted the schools to take soundings from the department, either directly or through myself or Neil. The fact was that many of the fee-paying schools had bad debts. During the boom years, enrolments in most had increased, as parents had more disposable income, but come the recession, collecting fees was becoming more and more of a problem. Now some were considering taking the same path as Wilson's Hospital in County Westmeath, which had joined the free scheme a couple of years earlier in order to ensure that it could retain its ethos and continue to serve its traditional pupil base, particularly the Church of Ireland community.

Wilson's Hospital started getting calls for advice and information from others who were interested in doing the same. At one stage, there were over a dozen or so schools either kicking the tyres or engaged in more serious and detailed discussions with the department about what joining the scheme would mean for them. It was largely uncharted territory for the department, which had to deal with issues such as the debt overhang in some schools, the ongoing costs associated with listed buildings, what to do with the extra staff and the teachers who didn't make the Teaching Council regulations for payment from the state, what should be the maximum fee allowed for boarding charges, what transition arrangements were necessary, and so on.

The basic principle governing discussions with any school considering entering the free scheme was straightforward – was the school needed? In the case of Kilkenny College, this was simple enough to answer, as it was the only school catering for the Protestant community across a wide area. The principal, Ian Coombes, said the historic switch-over had saved the struggling school from laying off any of its teachers. 'It enables us to press ahead with curricular developments and our building development plans,' he added. Kilkenny

College reported that falling incomes and rising taxes had made it more difficult for families to send their children to fee-paying schools. The reduction in state aid was also clearly a factor in its decision to join.

Similar reasons prompted the country's only Quaker school, Newtown School in Waterford, to open belated and urgent discussions with the department, which resulted in a quick turnaround to their fortunes and their entry into the free scheme from September 2014. The principal, Keith Lemon, said pressure on families to meet tuition fees of over €6,000 had been a big factor in the move. 'The truth of the matter is more and more parents have been struggling to pay the fees for their children to attend our school,' said Mr Lemon. 'Moving to the free-education system opens the school to more students while reducing the amount of money it costs for them to be educated here.'

Meanwhile, in Dublin, no Minister for Education could preside over the closure of the country's oldest secondary school, St Patrick's Cathedral Grammar School, which has a fine choral tradition but was facing financial difficulties. It also joined the scheme, as did Gormanston College in County Meath, where the numbers of pupils had fallen to worrying levels. It failed the 'Is the school needed?' principle based on current requirements for places, but a significant number of additional post-primary places will be required over the next few years because of the burgeoning population in the sur-rounding area. Rather than wait for years and watch land prices rise, the department decided to avail itself of the opportunity to welcome the college into the free scheme. Its golfing pupils must be delighted, as it is the only school in the free scheme with a nine-hole course.

Publication of Martin Hanevy's report in early March

2013 had little or nothing to do directly with the discussions we were having with schools about joining the scheme. Nor, strangely, did it galvanize the Labour Party into stepping up its demands for hitting them hard. In fact, having made such a big deal about fee-paying schools in 2011 and 2012, Labour suddenly dropped the issue for the rest of 2013, for no apparent reason other than, perhaps, a realization that they weren't going to get any more change immediately out of Fine Gael on the question. But it's an issue that hasn't gone away and will surface again publicly. Some backbenchers are already beginning to make noises that should worry the fee-paying school sector.

15. The biggest shake-up ever of school-entrance rules

Shortly after Ruairi came into office we discovered that proposals to reform school enrolment policies were already well advanced in the department. He endorsed them in a lukewarm fashion to begin with, but was soon persuaded by his team that this could prove to be his greatest achievement – his greatest legacy, I called it. We immediately saw the proposals' potential significance for making schools more inclusive and for breaking the old-boy and old-girl network that still characterizes much of Irish society.

Martin Hanevy had led the team working on the proposals. He can be stubborn at times, but he has a strong egalitarian streak. The changes would make it much more difficult for either primary or secondary schools to refuse to enrol their fair share of special-needs pupils and would outlaw the charging of fees for applications. We knew they were fraught politically and that we would face an uphill battle to get them over the line.

Schools' admission policies are a contentious area in many countries. In Ireland, it's a bit like the CAO, where the only fair system is the one that gets your daughter or son into their first choice. In Ireland, about 80 per cent of schools are able to take all-comers, but the problems arise in the other 20 per cent which are oversubscribed. Long waiting lists for some Dublin secondary schools are commonplace – there is an apocryphal story of an expectant mother who turned up with a scan to put down her unborn and unnamed daughter on the waiting list for a school in South County Dublin. Every now and then, news stories appear of parents queuing all night to get their children's name down for a particular school. Stories also began appearing some years back about newcomers to the country encountering great difficulties in getting their children into any school.

Many parents of children with special needs have stories of being encouraged to take their children to another school with 'better facilities'. An audit of schools in 2008 had suggested this practice was common, even if there was no evidence of systematic – or, as it was termed, 'problematic' – discrimination.

Minister Mary Hanafin, who had commissioned the report at the time, said that she had resisted public pressure 'to name and shame schools' with restrictive admission policies. But she did mention an unnamed girls' school in the west where just 0.5 per cent of students were foreign nationals, and another unnamed girls' school in the mid-west that had no special-needs provision. In both cases, she said, the audit indicated that other schools in the respective areas had above-average provision for newcomer children and special-needs students. It was clearly time to introduce a more transparent system, and that's what the department had been working on when we arrived.

In June 2011, Ruairi published a discussion document setting out options for consideration to make the system fairer. These included abolishing waiting lists and the practice of first come, first served, both of which made it more difficult for newcomers – either from abroad or from different parts of the country – to get a place for their children. Other options mentioned were removal of the practice of giving priority to a student on the basis of being a relative of a staff member, a member of the board of management, a past pupil or a benefactor of the school. The last two options particularly exercised some South Dublin schools, which argued that past pupils would no longer contribute generously to their old school if there was no guarantee that their children could get a place in their pater's or ma's old alma mater, and this would seriously hamper their fund-raising arrangements to improve the school's facilities.

The *gaelscoileanna* were upset over the suggestion of replacing requirements for competency of parents in a particular language with a criterion that parents should respect the linguistic policy of the school. The belief was that some *gaelscoileanna* were refusing to admit pupils whose parents were not proficient in the Irish language, including non-native Irish, and the proposal was to change that. There were also predictable criticisms of the suggestion that admission should not be contingent on the payment of a booking deposit on the basis that there was cost involved to the school in processing the applications.

The document further suggested that regulations could standardize time frames for enrolment, notification requirements, application and decision-making processes and the appeals process. It also set out possible new sanctions in a case where a school or board of management was not compliant with any new regulations. In such cases, a patron or the minister could have the power to appoint an external admissions officer and remove the control of enrolment from a board. This was radical stuff indeed.

Predictably, there was a huge reaction to the document, which was followed in September 2012 by the framework for further discussion ahead of enacting legislation. It is not generally the case that draft regulations are provided along-side a bill, but in this case Ruairi wanted to encourage a comprehensive discussion on the proposed measures. The bill and draft regulations were referred to the Oireachtas Joint Committee on Education and Social Protection to allow a full public discussion. The committee invited written submissions, and a total of fifty-seven were received.

In the subsequent public hearings it was clear that commit-tee members favoured a full ban on reserving places for children of past pupils, but that game was being played else-where. All this time, behind the scenes, lobbying was taking place at various levels to soften what was proposed, including direct approaches to the Taoiseach's office, which we heard about. After a while the fee-paying schools convinced Ruairi to drop the complete ban on priority for children of past pupils and replace it with provision to allow them to retain up to a quarter of their places for the sons and daughters of former pupils. Meanwhile, the *gaelscoileanna* successfully put pressure on Eamon Gilmore, a fluent Irish speaker, to allow them to insist that parents of children enrolling in their schools had to have some proficiency in the language. The ban on priority for children of staff was also lifted – the numbers involved were not massive and Gilmore didn't want to annoy teachers unnecessarily. It could have meant severe disruption for some families if teacher parents had to bring their children to one school before heading to work in another. Gilmore's people conveyed his views to us, and we accommodated them in the redrafting.

The draft memo for the Cabinet and revised bill and regu-lations also faced delays, because of discussions with Fine Gael, which was alarmed over what some of its advisers saw as interference in the autonomy of schools. This was made clear at a number of bilaterals and in conversations between our people and the Taoiseach's advisers, especially Andrew McDowell. It was a view shared by the secondary-schools managers' body, the Joint Managerial Body, whose general secretary, Ferdia Kelly, said that Ruairi was trying to micromanage the enrolment process in a way that was unnecessary.

Mark Kennelly told me he believed that enrolment policy was part of Ruairi's 'secularist agenda'. If he really believed that, it was seriously worrying, as he had a major influence on the Taoiseach. Department officials were concerned that such a view would seriously be entertained by such a senior adviser who is so close to the head of government.

In March, the Taoiseach's advisers pulled Ruairi's memo from cCabinet because they said it would cause problems for the Fine Gael backbenchers. This infuriated Ruairi. Labour ministers always have their own session before the Cabinet meets. After telling them what had happened, Ruairi walked into the full Cabinet meeting with twenty copies of the memo under his arm, the first time he had ever done so. But the Taoiseach ruled out late memos that day, as both Joan Burton and Michael Noonan also wanted to get late additions on to the agenda. However, he did agree to Ruairi giving a flavour of the bill to the teachers' conferences two weeks later, where it attracted huge coverage again.

Ruairi got his memo through the Cabinet shortly after that and published the Education (Admissions to Schools) Bill 2013 at the end of August that year. It was described by Katherine Donnelly in the *Irish Independent* as the biggest shake-up ever of school-entrance rules. It was an impressive list of changes: no more waiting lists (enrolment would open on 1 October of the preceding year); no more 'administration' or 'booking' fees; no pre-enrolment interviews of parents or children; a limit of 25 per cent on the number of past pupils' children a school could enrol in any school year; and a simplified school-level arrangement for enrolment appeals.

It was a long and intense journey to get to publication of the bill. And it's not finished yet. Publishing a bill and getting it enacted and implemented are different stages in the process. Despite his impatience to see his new enrolment policies in place, Ruairi was gone from office before that happened, and it was left to his successor, Jan O'Sullivan, to proceed with it, which she clearly wanted to do. 'I'm inclined to be as inclusive as I possibly can. My preference is for schools that have mixed abilities and mixed social classes,' she was quoted as saying in the *Sunday Times* in August 2014. But she also said that she wanted to look again at the derogation which would allow some schools to allocate up to 25 per cent of their places to children of past pupils. The phrase 'some schools' is code for those in the fee-paying sector. There are a few more twists and turns left on this particular subject.

16. '*Tá sé ag éisteacht*'

Muammar Gaddafi's death in Libya in October 2011 over-shadowed every other news story of the day. And it saved us from hugely embarrassing front-page U-turn headlines over Junior Cert reform. It was to be the first of a number of reversals of fortune in what Ruairí hoped would be his lasting contribution to Irish education.

Even before he came into office, Ruairí was completely sold on the idea of reform at the junior-cycle level and this was put into the Programme for Government. But his eagerness to push it through got him into trouble on a couple of occasions.

The need for change was obvious. It was shown in the ESRI longitudinal study of nine hundred students which highlighted concerns about students being overstressed, and taking ten to fifteen subjects in the Junior Cert. The same report also revealed worrying evidence of significant numbers of students becoming 'disengaged' in their second year. As Ruairí would regularly say, too many students, and particularly boys and those from working-class backgrounds, 'have already entered the departure lounge' by that stage. They may drop out or remain in school, but they are not engaged with a system that does not suit them. That's five or six thousand young people who start secondary school and do not stay for the full five or six years. Just over 90 per cent of young people are staying on to the Leaving Cert, which is high by international standards. A nationally certified exam taken at fifteen or sixteen years of age, such as the fore-runners to the Junior Cert, the Group Cert or the Inter Cert, was designed for a different era, when most young people's education came to a full stop at that age. In Finland, they don't take an externally marked exam until they are eighteen.

Fortunately, the groundwork had been done by the NCCA, which advises on curricular changes. Its chief executive, Dr Anne Looney, had been pushing for reform at both Junior and Leaving Certificate levels for years. But she was becoming frustrated at the lack of encouragement from successive ministers. In 2007, the council had proposed an ambitious three-year rolling programme for the Leaving Certificate, which would cost more than €50 million to implement. But the minister of the day, Mary Hanafin, had dubbed this the 'Rolls-Royce option' for exam reform and sought instead to establish less ambitious practical reforms, such as changes to the timetable. Dr Looney's term of office in the NCCA was nearly up, and she figured there was no point in seeking another term unless she got a clear signal that the new minister was serious about curricular and assessment reform. That message was conveyed through an intermediary, and I sent back the clear assurance that, yes, we were serious about change.

Ruairi appreciated there was no point in reforming the Leaving Cert – whatever about the points system – without first changing the Junior Cert. He basically endorsed what the NCCA was proposing, which was to shift the way students learned from a largely passive model to one that was more interactive, and the way in which they were assessed from a written exam at the end of three years to a greater element of assessment in schools by their own teachers. He welcomed the emphasis on the dialogue between student and teacher in the learning process. And he endorsed the focus on assessment that was more holistic, more designed to capture the students' individual strengths and to allow those strengths to be built upon. Students themselves clearly wanted change. This was shown in the consultation process organized by the NCCA, the Office of the Minister for Children and Youth Affairs, and the Dáil na nÓg Council (the national parliament for young people aged between twelve and eighteen, under the umbrella of the Department of Children and Youth Affairs). The comment of one student was telling – 'You can't put three years' work into a few hours.'

The NCCA proposals included a limit of eight subjects for students taking the exam. Initially, Ruairi wanted that limit to apply for students entering their first year in 2012 and 2013, but this caused the first of the many rows that were ahead of us. Schools wanted it delayed at least until the major changes began in 2014. He agreed to postpone the start date and to make the announcement in October at the annual conference of the National Association of Principals and Deputy Principals (NAPD), whose director, Clive Byrne, was an enthusiastic supporter of Junior Cert change. I inserted a line *as Gaeilge* in Ruairi's speech, which was probably the only time he uttered any words in Irish in forty months as Minister for Education and Skills. Referring to the picture of himself on the NAPD newsletter that was captioned '*Tá sé ag éisteacht*', he said that he was indeed listening and taking on board the principals' concerns about introducing a limit on the number of subjects too early. 'I have listened to those concerns. As the caption on the cover of your executive's newsletter said, "*Tá sé ag éisteacht*." I therefore welcome this opportunity to address those concerns.'

He then proved he had been listening by making the announcement about the eight-subjects limit being delayed until 2014. Managers and unions, whom I had tipped off in advance, welcomed the decision. But it was undoubtedly a climbdown. The U-turn just happened to come on the same day that Gaddafi was killed, to inevitable quips afterwards that we had arranged to get the Libyan dictator bumped off in order keep Ruairi off the front pages.

The change bought time but no sign of agreement from the unions, which were worried about the prospect of some element of school-based assessment – in other words, teachers assessing their own students. In April 2012, Moira Leydon, the Association of Secondary Teachers Ireland's progressive education and research officer, was replaced on the NCCA by Philip Irwin, an ASTI hard-liner and currently president of the union. It was a setback, as Leydon was certainly more open to the idea of teachers assessing their own students for exam purposes than Irwin – she was not reappointed to the council, probably because of that openness.

Over the next few months, the details of how the assessment would work were fleshed out in bold detail. The unions were wary of what was coming and continued to make clear their opposition to some form of school-based assessment. At a political level, there was no great pressure, apart from Fianna Fáil urging us to listen to the unions. And bold is the only way to describe what Ruairi, the officials and advisers were talking about – effectively, an end to the Junior Cert as we know it. Clive Byrne of the principals' association, whom Ruairi had appointed to the NCCA in March 2012, did some useful groundwork (though he did it wearing his NAPD hat). After the Junior Cert results were released in September, he wrote an article in the *Examiner* saying that, while the planned reforms of the three-year junior cycle were aimed at making the exam less high-stakes, things could be taken further. 'If we're in the middle of reforming it to ensure it's not a high-stakes exam any more, why not be a bit more courageous? The idea is to see if we could diminish the effect of exams on students by having them corrected by their own teachers, who would make professional judgements and offer direct feedback.'

On 2 October, Ruairi briefed his Cabinet colleagues on what was coming. It was one of three memos dealing with education that day; the others dealt with the Education and Training Boards and with draft legislation to stop universities paying over the odds in terms of government-approved salaries and allowances, as happened in too many cases. Ruairi received a lot of support from colleagues for what he was doing on junior-cycle reform. That particular Cabinet meeting didn't have a long agenda; in fact, the paucity of items was noted and criticized the previous day by Colm O'Reardon. We tried to keep the details of what we were planning under wraps until the day of the announcement on 4 October 2012, but Sean Flynn got enough information to write a story for the *Irish Times* which would have thrown a spanner in the works. I convinced him to delay publishing the story until the day of the launch, which he agreed to do in return for more details. We were happy to supply them, and I even helped write part of the story for Sean, much to the bemusement and surprise of some senior officials.

The front-page *Irish Times* exclusive story set the tone for a positive media treatment of the dramatic changes in store. Instead of a written exam at the end of three years, all subjects would have school-based assessment, which would be worth 40 per cent of the marks, and a written exam worth 60 per cent. The schoolwork component would be based on work completed by the student during their second and third years and would be marked by the teacher in the school using a supplied marking guide. The kinds of work involved would include assignments, projects, cases studies, performances, oral activities, written pieces and tests of different kinds. Schools could use portfolios if they wished. The final assessment component would be a single written paper or assignment. In the first few years of implementation, the papers would be set by the State Examinations Commission (SEC) but administered and, for the most part, corrected by teachers as part of their assessment of students. However, in the case of English, Irish and mathematics, the papers would also be corrected by the SEC for an introductory transition period.

This was far-reaching stuff indeed and was well received by school principals, employer and business groups, virtually all media commentators and, it seemed, by most of the public. The exception was the post-primary teacher unions, particularly the ASTI. Its representative on the NCCA, Philip Irwin, was at a seminar the morning of the announcement in the Clock Tower on the department's campus, where the distinguished education academic Professor Paul Black, from King's College in London, was talking about the value of teachers assessing their own students. Irwin challenged the guest speaker, telling him that he lived in a monarchy, whereas Irish people lived in a republic which was corrupt in everything except for state-run exams. Black interrupted him and said he would not tolerate such an attack on the professionalism of teachers, to applause from many in the audience. Indeed, some argued that this was one of the weaknesses in the unions' opposition to assessing their own students. Their fear was that they would come under pressure to mark up certain pupils and they said that their role would change from being an advocate for the pupil to that of a judge.

The ASTI argument would certainly have a lot of validity if we were talking about teachers marking their own students for the Leaving Certificate, but the discussion was about a low-stakes exam instead. Teachers in other countries already assessed their own students for exam purposes without being vulnerable to bribery, as was suggested would happen here. At home, teachers and lecturers assessed and marked their students for national post-Leaving Certificate courses, in the institutes of technology, in the universities and other institutions, with no alarm being sounded about corruption or pressure. That aspect of the debate rumbled on, but the newspapers showed no interest in figures we produced on the number of TUI and ASTI members already engaged in assessing their own students for state exams.

By coincidence, a name from the past had popped up on RTÉ Radio One the morning Ruairí was announcing these controversial reforms. At 6.40 a.m. I was astonished to hear the voice of Paul Andrews SJ giving his 'Thought for the Day'. Fr Paul was one of the heroes of the education-reform movement that had made some limited headway forty years previously. In the mid-seventies, he had headed up a representative committee that issued a report calling for far-reaching changes in the teaching and assessment of the junior cycle. The wheels of justice are said to grind slowly. Well, education reform can take even longer, and it was not until 1992 that the Group Certificate, which was mainly offered in vocational schools, merged with the Intermediate Certificate to become the Junior Certificate. Unfortunately, that's all that happened at that time, as the modes of assessment didn't change – a reform effectively killed off by the teaching unions, the ASTI in particular. I made contact with Fr Paul a few days later and he wished us well with Ruairi's reforms, even if he was sceptical about how far we could push them. By now eighty-five, he had been around the block and seen and heard a lot over the years, so I took his warning to heart. And, sure enough, as events unfolded, Fr Paul's scepticism was warranted.

Throughout 2013 and into 2014, increasingly angry noises were being made by the two secondary teachers' unions, the ASTI and the TUI, as they tried to gazump each other in terms of militancy with threats of strikes, non-cooperation and protests, and so on. And it wasn't just the unions. The History Teachers' Association was also stepping up its campaign and was getting places in convincing people that history would disappear from the curriculum. We didn't believe that would happen, and neither did most school principals.

We were getting plenty of positive media support for the reforms, but public and even political support was beginning to ebb. In June 2013, there was a surprising discussion out of the blue about the junior cycle at a normal special advisers' meeting, with Colm O'Reardon from the Tánaiste's office saying he wasn't happy with the whole project and that he wondered where it was going, particularly with history. He wanted history retained as a compulsory subject, but I had to point out that it was compulsory for only half the schools – the traditional voluntary secondary schools. It wasn't compulsory in community schools and colleges, comprehensive schools or vocational schools, yet most students took the subject in those schools, and we were convinced this would remain the position for all schools. It was an inconclusive discussion, but I mentioned it to my colleagues and officials back in the department as another indication that we were up against it in terms of the PR battle with historians and the History Teachers' Association of Ireland.

Ruairi was determined to press on despite the growing opposition from the unions, and plenty of meetings took place within the department on aspects of the planned changes. One of the trickiest decisions was what name to use once the Junior Certificate was gone. The NCCA suggested a number of options, including An TT (i.e. An Teastas Táirsí – the Gateway Certificate, as they translated it), which we rightly derided. Nor were the possibilities put forward by the Irish Second-level Students Union much better. They included School-based Teacher-led Assessment and Reporting System (STARS), Irish Comprehensive/Certificate Assessment (ICA) and, my favourite, Innovation Relevant Assessment – or IRA for short (a gratifying sign of the success of the peace process, perhaps, that the young people in ISSU did not see a difficulty with this acronym). Ruairi didn't like any of them and started drawing up his own list of possibilities. In January 2014, he announced the new name – Junior Cycle Student Award (JCSA).

Talks with the unions on the junior cycle stuttered along, but they were getting nowhere, partly because they were a sideshow to the main act, which was about teachers' pay and allowances, which were about to be slashed by the government. While there was genuine opposition to Ruairi's reforms, some of it was fuelled by anger over pay and allowances. It became a proxy issue. It was frustrating, and it was hard to see where progress would be made. Our gloom about progressing the reform made us slightly edgy. There was great amusement when the TUI president, Gerry Craughwell, left a meeting in the department and in a bullish interview on RTÉ declared, 'We looked for three things and got neither of them.' The moment of light relief was fleeting.

In January 2014, Ruairi set up a National Working Group to explore issues of concern to the various education partners about the JCSA, but the unions played little part. In March, both unions protested over the changes and a petition was signed by almost ten thousand of the ASTI's eighteen thousand members opposed to his plans. Ruairi gave a tough speech to the ASTI convention in Wexford at Easter, inviting teachers to play a more meaningful role in the talks. But they were in no mood to listen. Members were directed not to take part in any training, school-planning, meetings or other activities connected to the new award. Matters got worse as plans were made for ballots on strike action.

From early 2014, the pressure from the unions continued to build on Ruairi to compromise on the changes and cut a deal. All of the political parties had endorsed the thrust of the junior-cycle changes, so they couldn't really call for them to be scrapped. This didn't stop Fianna Fáil's education spokesperson, Charlie McConalogue, from laying into Ruairi and saying things such as that the concerns of teachers and independent experts could not continue to be ignored. But it was unclear whether the unions were actually minded to accept any form of compromise, and we were concerned that any concessions offered to them would simply be pocketed in the event of a reshuffle, with a new minister facing a changed set of demands from them to further dilute the proposals.

Jan O'Sullivan made it clear from the beginning that she was equally determined to press ahead with the junior-cycle changes, and didn't meet the teaching unions until the start of September 2014, after the revised English curriculum had been introduced into all schools. The reform train had left the station.

17. Megaphone diplomacy

We never thought we would be so delighted to see a protestor, especially one with a megaphone. 'He's saved the day for us,' I said to myself at the 2014 secondary teachers' convention in Wexford, where he had started to bellow at the minister over pay and cuts.

Ruairi had put his foot in it at the Irish National Teachers' Organisation congress that morning by going off script when talking about raising the entry requirement for teacher training to higher-level C in maths and coming out with an ill-judged aside about knowing he was talking to a 'highly feminized audience and profession'. This drew jeers from delegates, and he lost the room.

What he was trying to say – though he didn't explain it well or get the chance to spell out his thinking in sufficient detail – was that research showed that female students tended to drop honours maths for Leaving Cert. (In many cases, it was probably a practical decision, to do with reducing workload, rather than to do with a student's capacity to study the subject.) But if it was made a requirement of entry into primary-school teaching, then more of them – who he believed were perfectly capable of doing the honours course – would stay studying at the higher level. He was not trying to say that girls were avoiding honours maths because they couldn't hack it, and these were the same people who had ended up going into teaching. Nor, indeed, was he saying that if someone was not able for the honours course they were of lesser intellectual capacity. But he was saying that to raise the overall standards of maths teaching in schools, those entering the profession – male or female – needed to have a strong background in maths.

He handed Sheila Nunan, the INTO general secretary, an ideal opportunity to have the obligatory pop at the minister without getting into a serious row. And she rose to it by saying, to huge applause, that it was the boys who *did* the honours maths [that] led the country to ruination. The story was already making waves on the radio and was likely to dominate the next day's papers. Enter the megaphone man – Andrew Phelan, a teacher in Lucan, County Dublin – at the ASTI convention, who would grab the headlines for days afterwards. We joked among ourselves that he should be instantly promoted by way of thanks.

The megaphone diplomat in Wexford was accompanied by incessant shouts and jeers throughout Ruairi's speech. It wasn't the first time Ruairi had encountered teachers' anger at the annual conferences, nor the first time the teachers were under fire for their protests, captured in the *Star*'s headline the previous year: 'Roaring at Ruairi'.

There is no doubt that the coverage of teachers and their conferences has been more critical in recent years, certainly much more so than when I was starting in educational journalism. I've attended conferences for forty-three years and have seen the commentary shift slowly but dramatically. Now, instead of unquestioning reportage, there is more emphasis on news stories and commentary, sometimes quite tough commentary. The criticism more often than not comes from opinion columnists such Emer O'Kelly or Kevin Myers rather than the education correspondents. After the 2013 conferences, Myers wrote a piece in the *Indo* where he laid into the unions over their attacks on Ruairi and concluded: 'I merely ask these questions: I lack the courage to offer any commentary on the pictures from conferences organized by unions named after, respectively, a preposition, the first half of an Italian sparkling wine and what appears to be an obscure French pronoun: namely, INTO, ASTI and TUI.' The arch, mocking tone said everything about his feelings for the unions.

The unions' anger is partly explained by cuts to pay and allowances in recent years. However, the reality is that the allowances bill for qualifications and promotions was growing exponentially and had to be capped. The fact that half the second-level teaching force were in promoted posts which attracted higher allowances didn't help. Teachers were a significant target in Brendan Howlin's first look at allowances in 2012. A review of all allowances and premium payments throughout the public service was commissioned – over a thousand of them in all, spread across the service. Many of them were arcane and were introduced decades earlier to solve some long-forgotten industrial-relations problem at the time. In education, I discovered there was something called a 'sleepover' allowance in some VEC centres for non-teaching staff (although I could never figure out who actually got it) and that there was some kind of payment for staff in one university – presumably Trinity – who prepared the ground for cricket matches.

Brendan Howlin suffered a rare political setback when his initial attempt to cut allowances failed miserably at the end of 2012. A further attempt to cut a deal on pay and allowances the following year also failed, when the unions narrowly voted to reject the Croke Park II pay deal. But Howlin's political fortunes revived later, when a subsequent version, the

Haddington Road Agreement, was accepted. The ASTI was one of the last unions to sign up, reluctantly. I had attended some of the meetings in the Department of Public Expenditure and Reform, and they were tough negotiations. The big revelation for me was the lack of sympathy for teachers there, except, perhaps, for young graduates who spent years subbing before they got a permanent job. Why should teachers get an extra allowance for a qualification they needed to have to join the profession anyway, DPER wanted to know, and with some validity. We argued that if allowances were to go then we needed a higher starting salary for new teachers than DPER was prepared to offer.

The animosity towards teachers in DPER made negotiations more difficult. It was doubly so because of the view also expressed at one DPER meeting that Department of Education officials were 'in thrall to the unions and not living in the real world', a perception that may come as something of a surprise to teacher unions. DPER knew there wouldn't be a huge amount of sympathy from the public for teachers if their allowances were cut. And if they took industrial action they would really be out in the public cold. A young teacher's complaint on radio that she couldn't possibly survive on a 'pittance' of a starting salary of €32,200 in a permanent job cut little ice with people who had no jobs or with graduates beginning their careers in temporary work or on lower salaries. Lots of people knew teachers – admittedly, probably teachers who had been in the profession for some years – whose situation was more secure and comfortable than that of workers in other public services and the private sector. I was astounded to meet a teacher and her university-lecturer husband at a party who between them earned the best part of €160,000, if not more, and were absolutely furious with Labour because their pay was cut. They said they would never vote for the party again. Didn't they know what was happening in the real world, where people in the private sector were either losing jobs or facing salary cuts? I wondered. When pressed, they admitted they weren't going to vote for Fine Gael either, who were 'worse', or for Fianna Fáil, who had caused the country's economic problems, and then realized they were running out of options unless they voted for Sinn Féin, the Socialists, People before Profit or independents, which seemed unlikely.

A negative view of teachers also makes it easier for a government to try to push through other types of changes – for instance, league tables, which come up in discussions at various levels now and then. They have been opposed by the department. I was surprised at the support among some of the Tánaiste's advisers for the publication of league tables of exam results, an idea that appeals to many in Fine Gael. Support for both ideas seems to stem largely from events in the UK. It's an idea that's anathema to many in Irish education who say league tables have damaged education in England and elsewhere.

Before coming to power in 1997, many in the Labour Party in Britain pledged to scrap league tables. Once in power, New Labour realized that league tables did create the appearance of accountability and were very popular with parents. For all their faults, they are still being published year after year in the UK. So far, the introduction of such league tables has been resisted in Ireland, and for good educational reasons. But we have come much closer to changing that position than teachers may realize. A similar political demand could develop here in time.

The related notion of formal appraisal of teachers, and

the idea of granting school principals greater autonomy in determining their own student–teacher ratios and pay levels for their staff are also gaining some currency in certain quarters, as they have elsewhere. If such changes come about – largely undesirable to members of the post-primary unions – the union members will have to blame themselves for allowing hard-liners to dictate the pace of educational discussion and ultimately lowering the status and bargaining power of the profession.

The protests in 2014 contrasted greatly with the reception Ruairi received in his first round of conferences at Easter 2011, when teachers listened, politely for the most part, to him talk about the dire state of the economy. When the coalition parties swept to power he was the first minister constantly to remind people that the country had lost its economic sovereignty and that Michael Collins, the state's first Minister for Finance, had more room for manoeuvre in 1922 than had Michael Noonan in 2011. As he was in the relatively unusual position as an education minister of once having had the finance brief, he had a more nuanced appreciation of the fiscal crisis than might have been expected. It was a bit of a cultural change for teachers' conferences, which were more used to ministers arriving with 'goodies' in the form of more jobs or resources for schools.

Up to mid-2011, ministers had official cars and officially appointed garda drivers who could legally break the speed limit if necessary. On the second day of the 2011 conferences, we had to get from Tralee to Cork quickly. We had been delayed when we stopped for an RTÉ radio interview over the phone, and then for coffee, where a couple of teachers approached and were delighted to tell the new minister what a great job he was doing and how he could do it even better. Back on the road after coffee, the driver put down the boot, touching 180kmh at one stage, only for a squad car to come chasing after us. Our driver put on the special blue hazard lights to indicate it was a state car and the garda car peeled away. Shortly after that the official cars were taken away and ministers had to make their own arrangements for cars and drivers. They also had to obey the speed limits.

In his first year in office, Ruairi's conference speeches were effectively written by a committee. The various sections in the department threw in their tuppence-ha'penny worth and then Ruairi added in his bit about the economy. The result was that the speeches were all over the place, trying to cover everything. This was the way it had been done for decades, but it was time to change and make them more focused. In our post mortem afterwards we agreed that there needed to be greater coherence to the speeches in future.

Speech writing is a particular art: you have to get the rhythm right for the speaker, avoid ambiguous or hard-to-pronounce words and be able to craft a message or several messages clearly and directly. After working with Neil Ward on a few speeches in those first few months we all soon realized that we had a very skilled speechwriter in our midst, and he was 'volunteered' for the job of taking responsibility for Ruairi's major speeches for the rest of his time in ministerial office. After a discussion with Ruairi on the issues he wanted raised, Neil would produce the first draft, circulate it to the various heads of the sections and fellow advisers, collate their feedback and that of Ruairi and produce a penultimate version, which we all looked at again before Ruairi signed it off.

The following year, 2012, Ruairi talked in detail about his

reform agenda and how the various elements knitted together. But when he tried the 'the country has lost its sovereignty' line again, and suggested that many in the education sector did not get the extent of the fiscal crisis, it didn't go down too well. People were tiring of austerity already. The INTO's press officer, Peter Mullan, later slagged me off for convincing Sean Flynn to carry a piece in his Teachers' Pet column in the *Irish Times* chastening teachers for their lack of interest in reforms outside their particular sector, and I retaliated by blaming him for Sean's reference to Ruairi's 'economics lecture'. We agreed it was fifteen-all.

Playing to the gallery is common at the conferences, and nothing moves delegates like a good, rousing, presidential attack on the minister of the day. TUI president Gerry Craughwell kept it up for the best part of an hour in 2013. He promised to keep it shorter in 2014, but he actually spoke for three minutes longer. It was good knockabout stuff, punctuated by thunderous applause from the delegates, which was in marked contrast to the unenthusiastic response to Ruairi's remarks on both occasions. Afterwards, Gerry said to me, 'Tell Ruairi it wasn't personal.' It may not have been, but it can be difficult to get back to 'just business as usual' the next day with the minister, advisers and officials. Ruairi didn't reveal his feelings one way or the other afterwards, but it couldn't have been easy sitting there for the best part of an hour taking a lot of abuse.

The conferences are attended by several department officials, who are there to support the minister, especially if he needs information for press queries, to gauge the mood of the conferences, meet and socialize with the union leaders and delegates. These same officials and, indeed, advisers would have formal meetings, negotiations and off-the-record talks with the union leaders on many issues over the following twelve months before the next round of conferences, so it was important to get to know them. As so often happens in negotiations, it's the personal and working relationships that make things happen and these are often forged over a late-night drink at such events.

It's not all beer, protests and angry speeches at the conferences. Other topics get an airing when surveys are produced on the effects of the latest cuts, and worries about the plight of part-time or temporary teachers are discussed, or fears about pensions and the like. And the delegates get through a lot of motions and speeches which don't attract the same attention as the protests and their complaints about pay and conditions. They discuss concerns about bullying, suicide, teenage drinking and drug taking, apprenticeships, underperformance by boys in exams, and so forth. It is a side of the conferences that demonstrates the genuine concern for and dedication to young people that commited teachers and union members have. Sometimes their concerns are not about education at all. The TUI, for instance, has a tradition of emergency motions on social issues at home or on conflicts in far-flung regions of the world. Not for nothing is it dubbed 'USI for adults'.

Sometimes the unions use the conferences to step up campaigns on particular issues. For instance, at the 2011 congress, the INTO was particularly vocal on the need to ensure that only qualified teachers would teach in the classroom. To bring that about, part of the Teaching Council Act, Section 30, would have to be officially 'commenced', or activated. Though the act dated from 2001, this part of it had been dormant, as neither the department nor outside interests had ever pursued it before. Once this provision was commenced, it would have the force of law and mean that only teachers who were registered with the Teaching Council could be paid out of state funds. Sounds simple, but it wasn't. The department had been dragging its heels on Section 30, but Ruairi was determined to implement it. We soon discovered all sorts of anomalies which could prevent some teachers, who had been paid out of the public purse for years, from continuing to draw a salary – everyone from swimming instructors in special-needs schools to teachers who were experts in particular fields of study but did not have full teaching qualifications.

Ruairi had a number of meetings with officials and with the director of the Teaching Council, Tomás Ó Ruairc, to ensure the momentum was kept up. A clever civil servant, Dalton Tattan, came up with a legal formula that would allow unqualified teachers to work for a few days in schools where it was impossible, in an emergency, to get a qualified teacher. It took longer than expected to get all suitably qualified teachers registered with the council and come up with a new classification of expert tutors who could continue to be paid. Bizarrely, we discovered that we couldn't meet the traditional legal requirement to print the commencement order on vellum paper, which had been unavailable for the previous year. So when Section 30 of the Teaching Council Act was signed, to bring it into operation Ruairi had to append his signature to heavy yellow paper.

We were anxious that Section 30 would be followed quickly by the commencement of the remaining sections of the Teaching Council Act, including those relating to teachers' continuing professional development and the council's investigative and disciplinary functions. The Medical Council has the power to investigate allegations of negligence by doctors under its Fitness to Practise procedure. The Teaching Council has a similar mechanism to sanction under-performing teachers – Fitness to Teach – which, like Section 30, had never been commenced. Ruairi was anxious that the first Fitness to Teach hearing would be held as soon as possible, to give parents the confidence that persistently under-performing teachers would be dealt with, and that persistent complaints would not be ignored. However, progress was slow in putting the mechanisms in place. It didn't happen under his watch.

Guest speakers at the teacher conferences can also lift teachers' vision and inspire them. One such brilliant choice was David Puttnam, who was at the ASTI convention in Cork in 2011. He spoke passionately about the use of technology in schools and struck up an immediate rapport with Ruairi. I was surprised to learn that Puttnam had been living in west Cork for more than twenty years. He has long been one of my heroes, both for his work in education and for his films, which include *The Killing Fields*. (Many years ago, I reported on the work that the relief agency Concern was doing in the refugee camps on the Thai border, home to tens of thousands of refugees from the dreaded Khmer Rouge in Cambodia. On two occasions, I reported from the camp featured in the film where the Cambodian journalist Dith Pran had arrived after a harrowing journey, so his story had a big impact on me.) Ruairi later invited Puttnam to Leinster House, and in December 2012 he was appointed by communications minister Pat Rabbitte as Ireland's first Digital Champion. A friendship developed between Ruairi and Puttnam, who was later to describe him as one of the two best ministers for education in the world he had ever come across. Wisely, he didn't choose a teacher conference to make the statement.

Going back to Ruairi's final conferences, at the ASTI convention he stuck to a script which had been designed to be tough. In the face of huge opposition, he entered the lion's den and spelled out very clearly his rationale for abolishing the Junior Cert. He also responded very directly to the criticisms of these reforms which had been levelled by the unions. Predictably, his speech went down very badly with the convention, but not as badly as the teachers' protests did with the general public. That night, a rebuke by the National Parents Council (Post-primary) of the protestors was the lead story on RTÉ television news and the second item was revealing footage of a brawl between moderate members of the union and the militant 'ASTI Fightback' group over how representative the group really was. Things were not helped by general secretary Pat King's remarks to the conference that he had been bullied and threatened online. He went on the Sean O'Rourke radio programme the next morning and apologized to Ruairi for the way he was treated and criticized the members of the union who had been so discourteous.

The moderates said they were 'sick' of the antics of the militants, but a young Dublin teacher responded by saying the education system was being dismantled under Pat King's leadership. 'They're doing nothing about it. We're all frustrated. They're standing by and watching it happen,' he said. What was really happening, though, was that the protestors were further damaging their own profession in the eyes of the wider public.

18. Looking for the quick wins

'High-minded reforms won't wash with the people,' Colm O'Reardon said, as he pressed us to come up with measures that would have more impact on ordinary parents. Ruairi's far-reaching structural reforms were all well and good, and, of course, strongly supported by the Tánaiste's team. But what they needed were some tangible wins, and quickly.

It was just months into the government's term, and already Labour's poll numbers were tumbling and the backbenchers were growing restive. I had argued that Ruairi's reform agenda should surely create some political capital, but they wanted to know how that could be translated into hard votes.

Jean O'Mahony reminded me that education hadn't saved the Greens from political annihilation. She was right. When the Greens were in coalition with Fianna Fáil, its deputies thought its work on education would help the party's electoral chances. Its education spokesperson, Paul Gogarty, was a colourful character and much of his political posturing was difficult to take seriously, but nobody doubted his interest in education, and when the Programme for Government was renegotiated in the autumn of 2009, the Greens, with Gogarty's pushing, were able to stitch in some protections for education. So, while other front-line services such as nursing were facing job losses, they succeeded in getting a guarantee that pupil–teacher ratios would be exempt. This was no mean achievement at a time when the country was sliding down the financial tubes.

But, as we were also rapidly discovering, protecting something from cuts didn't result in any electoral benefit. It made not a jot of difference to the Greens' electoral prospects sixteen months later, when the public turned against both government parties for landing the country in an economic mess. The Green Party lost all six of its Dáil seats.

Now Labour was also in trouble in the polls and protecting front-line teaching jobs was not enough. The Tánaiste's people were anxious to avoid following the Greens and wanted us to help capture support from the ordinary man and woman in the street, especially parents, who were facing high back-to-school costs.

Neil forwarded a number of ideas, such as a book-rental scheme, high-quality early-childhood education that would require better mandatory minimum qualifications for all pre-school workers and investment in additional inspectors with pre-school expertise, or shifting sports capital grants so that they could be shared between schools and local communities. I suggested a charter for parents, setting out their rights in education. It was agreed to work on the charter as well as on a school-book-rental scheme and to do something about the cost of school uniforms, which was a huge issue for parents.

The first area we tackled was school books, where we began looking at the idea of expanding rental schemes. It seemed the most sensible way to go, as we would never get enough money to give free school books to all, as they did in most other developed countries. We met the Irish Educational Publishers' Association in October 2011 to press for their cooperation. They represented the main players in the industry – an industry that is worth around €50 million. It turned out to be a memorable meeting in more ways than one.

The chief inspector, Dr Harold Hislop, reminded them that elsewhere in the economy prices were coming down to reflect the new economic reality. They said that they would give a discount to schools that set up book-rental schemes. We then moved on to the needless changes in textbooks, which drove parents mad, as they meant parents could not use second-hand books and had to buy new ones. Ruairi produced a book I had given him that had only minimal changes from an edition published a year or two earlier. They agreed to limit revisions and new editions within a four-year time frame. We would have liked longer, but were happy to take four.

We were making progress when, unexpectedly, a big row broke out between two of the publishers present. Other than offer to act as referees, we couldn't do very much on our side of the table, apart from wait to see how the fight played out.

Afterwards, we announced details of the Code of Conduct we had reached with the association on the reduction in prices for school-book-rental schemes and the promise to avoid making changes annually. We didn't leak details of the row between the publishers, but a version appeared a couple of weeks later in a daily newspaper which claimed, inaccurately, that it had got so heated that Ruairi and the rest of us vacated the room for a time to leave them at it. Nothing of the sort happened – we were more than happy to remain, as it was too good a spat to miss.

Meanwhile, Ian O'Mara had written a useful paper on what it would cost to extend rental schemes to all primary and post-primary schools. Such schemes would certainly reduce the back-to-school costs for parents. Guidelines for schools on setting up such schemes had been written by Dr Hislop, and suggested that the average cost for a parent of a primary-school child could be reduced from over €100 to a token €20 to participate in a book-rental scheme each year. Many primary schools and a smaller percentage of post-primary schools already had them, but we wanted to extend their reach.

We thought we could get money from Joan Burton in Social Protection. She initially indicated she was agreeable to transferring some of her Back to School money for such a measure for the 2013 budget. In the end, that didn't happen – in the run-up to budgets, such options regularly appear on the table, but transfers from one department to another happen very rarely. During 2013, the issue was still under active consideration at Labour adviser level. Jean O'Mahony wanted us to find €15 million from within our own spending to ensure book-rental schemes for all schools – an option that was never realistic, given the other spending pressures faced in education. (And we weren't the only ones under pressure. James Reilly was looking for supplementary budgets yet again, and Brendan Howlin was at loggerheads with him trying to get him to control health spending. Also, unemployment wasn't yet falling fast enough to help Joan Burton avoid similar pressure to find savings.)

However, in the last few days before the 2014 budget, we managed to get the money from Brendan Howlin as part of the funds raised from the sale of the National Lottery licence. So Ruairi was able to announce a three-year €15 million fund which would be targeted specifically at primary schools that did not currently operate a book-rental scheme. Schools that had put schemes in place, along with the INTO, reacted with fury, claiming that we were rewarding schools that hadn't bothered to help parents until that point and punishing those who had made greater effort. They were within their rights to complain, but we had to find some way to remove the inequity from the system that saw some parents able to bene-fit from book-rental schemes and others denied that chance to reduce their back-to-school costs. Also, we simply didn't have enough money initially to reward them all and wanted to get the reluctant schools to set up their own rental schemes.

As we had expected, giving increased funding to those who didn't have such schemes didn't consume all the money we had been allocated, so a couple of months later we dis-tributed the remainder, over €8 million, among schools with existing rental schemes. The increased funding was sold as another part of Ruairi's wider agenda to tackle the high school costs for parents.

School uniforms were our next issue. Ruairi upset the Irish school-uniform industry when he suggested the use of cheaper generic uniforms to which a crest could be attached. The industry accused him of threatening jobs at home, but tackling the issue was clearly popular with the public. The practice of schools making arrangements with one local sup-plier to sell crested uniforms was unpopular with many parents, who knew that generic uniforms were available in Tesco or Lidl at a fraction of the cost. The Irish school-uniform industry argued that these would be of lower quality, but Ruairi firmly believed that parents should have the right to make calls on quality versus cost themselves.

We issued a circular to schools in December 2013 telling them to conduct surveys of parents to find out if they wanted the school to have a uniform. If so, they were asked did they want a generic type or did they want a specific, bespoke one. Ruairi issued a statement saying that parents were the ones who had to bear the cost of school uniforms, so it was only right that they were given a role in deciding the type of uniform they had to pay for.

The Tánaiste's chief of staff, Mark Garrett, was particularly keen to use the issue to bolster Eamon Gilmore as the champion of struggling parents. The *Herald* carried a story saying that 'Tánaiste Eamon Gilmore is leading the school-uniforms proposal which would allow for generic uniforms to be purchased with a separate school crest that could be stitched or ironed on.' There were a couple of days where we had to argue with journalists that this was Ruairi's idea, and not that he was being forced to do it by the Tánaiste. By that stage, the Tánaiste was so badly in need of positive coverage that his advisers were willing to have a pop at other Labour ministers if necessary.

The *Herald* article also suggested that schools could face financial penalties if they refused to comply with proposed regulations allowing for cheaper uniforms instead of expensive crested jumpers and blazers. Penalties were never on the table, but that fact did not get in the way of some good spin.

We were told later by the Tánaiste's advisers that the uniform policy went down a treat with focus groups. So much so that the following month our press officer, Deirdre Grant, told us that they wanted another whirl around the school-uniforms story, although we had nothing new to say.

The ballots went ahead in many schools, and afterwards the National Parents Council (Primary) carried out its own survey to find out how they went. A disappointing number hadn't bothered to conduct the polls, or worse, if they did, in many cases parents were not informed of the outcome. So much for partnership with parents.

But there was more to the balloting exercise than met the eye. In trying to poll parents on the issue of school uniforms, we were clarifying our thinking on how we could press ahead with a charter for parents and what the level of interest would be. Ireland and other countries had seen the development of charters in public- and private-sector organizations in recent years. These charters set out what those in receipt of services could expect, and how those delivering the services accounted to the public for what they were providing. I had preliminary discussions with Áine Lynch, CEO of the National Parents Council (Primary), in June 2013 about what might go into a charter, and Neil picked up on these later. What she had in mind was some kind of framework that would allow for greater positive engagement of parents in their children's education at school level, in the community and at home.

Parents' rights in Ireland were enshrined in the constitution and in the 1998 Education Act, which sought to put the involvement of parents at the heart of the education system. In 2014, Ruairi spelled out his thinking at the INTO congress when he said that not enough had been done to underpin this involvement of parents in all aspects of education. He mentioned in particular Section 28 of the Act, which allowed for procedures to be implemented to support the expression of grievances by parents: 'Unfortunately, it has not been possible to give meaningful effect to that section of the act. But more troubling is that Section 28 does not set out principles on how schools should engage positively with parents, so that grievances are minimized.' Providing such principles in legislation would be a recognition 'that parents must have positive rights in relation to the operation of school', he said.

And he announced his plan to create a Parents' and Learners' Charter – putting the involvement of parents and students at the heart of how schools operated.

Ruairi did not remain in office long enough to see his idea through legislatively, but if the legislation proceeds, and is followed by a full Parents' and Learners' Charter, it will be a further part of his legacy. And as his party so badly wanted, it will be a reform that will be immediately apparent to parents, as schools will no longer have any choice but to put parental involvement at the heart of everything they do.

19. Revolt over special-needs cuts

If medical cards are the hot-button issue for health, then special needs is the equivalent for education. It took over two years, but when the row blew up in June 2013, it was short, sharp and all-consuming.

It started with an announcement on Wednesday, 19 June, from the National Council for Special Education (NCSE) that the resource hours for children with special needs would be cut from September. What was happening was simple; how to solve it wasn't. The number of approved applications for resource hours had gone up by 12 per cent. But, for budgetary reasons, the number of resource teachers – fully qualified teachers who specialized in helping those with special needs – had increased only slightly. To spread the number of teachers around all of those entitled to resource hours, we had to cut the amount of time each pupil got – again. It had been done over the previous two years, when a few minutes were shaved off the time they were given, and there was no public outcry. Nobody in the department or the NCSE was happy about the further reduction but there was really no option if we were to live within budget. However, this third cut was too much and the clamour was growing for a change in policy.

The proposed reduction in hours was the lead item on RTÉ, where it was denounced as 'savage' by the INTO. Eamon Gilmore had the misfortune of taking that day's Leaders' Questions, which was dominated by the issue. The cut was also the subject of a topical-issues debate later in the day. Mark Garrett was furious with us for allowing the announcement to be made on Gilmore's watch and tore strips off both myself and Neil, pulling us out of meetings – not once, but twice – to do so.

The backbenchers were in revolt as the story gathered momentum. Ruairi, and Neil as his political adviser, addressed – separately – hastily called meetings of Labour and Fine Gael TDs and senators, who were getting it in the neck from constituents. They demanded that we revert to the situation of three years earlier, before any hours were reduced. But to do that would mean the appointment of an extra 1,500 teachers and a cost of €130 million, which was impossible.

On Thursday and Friday, we had held emergency sessions at adviser level with the Tánaiste's people, who wanted us to change the 'narrative' on special needs, which was easier said than done. There was no shortage of empathy for pupils with special needs, just a shortage of money. We were already spending huge sums in this area – more than the country was spending on the gardaí and almost the same amount as was being spent across the entirety of higher education. But the fact that our spending in this area was so vast was just not getting across.

There was anecdotal evidence that the resources were not being put to best use and that middle-class parents who could afford to pay for private psychological reports were doing so and getting additional resource teaching hours for their children. While we couldn't accuse educational psychologists, parents clearly believed they got the advice they paid for. It's not that easy always to distinguish between specific, mild general and borderline general learning disabilities. In the case of special-needs assistants, there was clearer evidence that SNAs had not always been put to best use. Neil spent some time trawling through the NCSE website and came up with stats showing a sample of schools and their allocations of additional teachers and SNAs for special-needs pupils. It was obvious that some middle-class areas in Dublin had disproportionate levels compared with poorer areas. But that didn't particularly excite the media, who had the bit between their teeth, with Niall Murray in the *Examiner* leading the charge. The weekend papers were equally damning, with Brendan O'Connor in the *Sunday Independent* saying we were suggesting that his daughter, who had special needs, was not as important as others, and his colleague Emer O'Kelly attacking Labour over what was happening.

At the Cabinet committee on social policy meeting on Monday afternoon, the Taoiseach and his colleagues were furious. Children's minister Frances Fitzgerald wanted to know why the 12 per cent spike in applications; more than 42,500 students needed additional teaching support from September, compared with 38,400 pupils the previous year. Principal officer Jim Mulkerrins could not readily offer an explanation for the surge at that stage, which occurred at the same time as overall pupil enrolments had gone up by only 1.3 per cent. He was under even greater pressure to explain how the department planned to cope with the increase. He said that if the department was to live within its agreed budget and keep the cap on teacher numbers, the only way to do it was by reducing the amount of time individual pupils would have with resource teachers. As an official, Jim couldn't say it, and Ruairi didn't either, but the obvious thing was to point out that the education budget had been agreed by the Taoiseach and the other ministers seven months earlier. I felt

Ruairi should have come to Jim's rescue earlier, but he remained silent, for the most part.

The Taoiseach was clearly exercised and not just, he indicated, because somebody had told him they would never vote again for him as a result of what had happened. He was adamant. 'You can't take away from people what they already have.' He was determined, even steely, about it – the cuts in resource teaching hours for special-needs pupils had to be reversed. Phil Hogan, who sat beside him, was equally strong – reverse it.

After the Cabinet committee meeting Jan O'Sullivan sent an email to a parent saying she expected changes as a result of the meeting. She was right, of course – there would be a change: there was now such a head of steam that there had to be a change – but what exactly could we do? It was clear that what had been a bad few days would get a lot worse unless we had a response to a Fianna Fáil private member's motion due to be taken the next day.

That thought preoccupied Ruairi, the department's secretary general Seán Ó Foghlú, Jim Mulkerrins, other officials and advisers and the new chair of the NCSE, Eamon Stack, for the next few hours. We finished drafting a counter-motion at 10 p.m. and were back in at eight o'clock the following morning tweaking it further. What we worked out was how many extra teachers we would need – five hundred, as it turned out. But we had to get agreement from our own officials, as well as the Taoiseach's and Tánaiste's offices, on extra teaching posts, and have the draft counter-motion with the Labour ministers for their 9.30 pre-Cabinet meeting. In the meantime, our new press officer, Siobhán Creaton, who had replaced Deirdre Grant while she was on maternity leave, was busy drafting and redrafting the press release.

The counter-motion got through the Cabinet, and Neil went to brief some anxious backbenchers, who then came over on to the Ministerial Corridor to congratulate Ruairi. They followed him out through the door of the Department of the Taoiseach and down the front steps, where they surrounded Ruairi as he announced the appointment of extra teachers for special-needs pupils to the assembled journalists and TV cameras. I had suggested he take the line that it was a great day for special needs, which, indeed, it was.

You couldn't call it a moment of triumph, but it was a moment of political relief – which was almost the same thing in the circumstances. However, there was a sting in the tail. Ruairi had committed a major faux pas in allowing the back-benchers on to the steps of Government Buildings. This prevented Fine Gael from claiming they had forced a U-turn on a Labour minister. But the Taoiseach's chief of staff, Mark Kennelly, was incandescent when he rang to berate me for the use of Government Buildings for party-political purposes. Mark Garrett also ticked me off, but with less vehemence. Government press secretary Feargal Purcell told Siobhán it was absolutely forbidden and could never happen again. The newspaper business, from which she had come, must have seemed almost tranquil by comparison with days like this.

We may have come up with a political solution with the counter-motion, but there was a bit more media play in the story. Next day, Wednesday, 26 June, the *Examiner* was scathing about 'red-faced' Quinn's 'embarrassing U-turn', but we were spared in the *Indo*, which was making a well-deserved meal out of its latest revelations from the leaked Anglo Irish tapes. That morning, it quoted an Anglo official boasting about 'Another day, another billion.' Oh, to have that to spend on special needs, I thought.

Meanwhile, Emma O'Kelly spoke on RTÉ about a separate battle looming on special-needs assistants. Just what we needed. We discovered that the department was about to issue a circular either that day or the next about SNAs, so we pulled it for a few days, as we knew an SNA protest was taking place outside Leinster House that afternoon. The circular was routine but would prompt renewed fears of cuts in SNA support as well, even if that was not the intention.

Ruairi was not the only politician at the receiving end over special needs. Fianna Fáil leader Micheál Martin went over to Molesworth Street to join the SNA protest but had to withdraw when some of the crowd began chanting, 'Shame, shame, shame.' It was a hugely embarrassing retreat for him, back to the relative safety of Leinster House.

Politicians on all sides of the house had had a stark reminder, if one were needed, from the week's dramatic events: special-needs provisions, like medical cards, are a virtually untouchable area for cuts.

20. Rural Ireland fights back

Small schools are a big issue for Fine Gael. This was brought home to me vividly when Enda Kenny grabbed me in a playful headlock at a dinner in NUI Galway in March 2012 and said, 'What are ye doing to my small schools, anyway?'

The very notion of small schools touches a memory deep in the Irish psyche. Even if they've never read the book, the idea brings to mind the bucolic charm of Alice Taylor's *To School through the Fields* and the view that small is cosy, safe and unhurried. In many cases it is, but try telling that to parents in a rural area whose children have no choice but to put up with a 'bad' teacher for three years, and they might argue otherwise.

The Taoiseach's worries were expressed after months of speculation and protests about the future of small schools. He represents Mayo, a constituency with many small schools, some very close to one another.

In the budget in December 2011, Ruairí had raised the threshold of numbers of pupils that small schools would need in order to take on a second, third or fourth teacher. The changes would be phased in over a three-year period, finishing in September 2014. Even with the changes, classes in these schools would continue to be smaller than most classes in urban areas. But the changes had heightened fears in many rural communities about the future of their schools – particularly when linked to anxieties about the closure of rural garda stations and post offices, and the downgrading of A&E services in some regional hospitals. The budget move led to protests outside Leinster House against 'cuts to small schools' in early February 2012. These coincided with a Dáil debate on a Fianna Fáil motion condemning the changes.

Neil had heard that the Fianna Fáil motion was being tabled on the previous Friday. He drafted the government counter-motion, which was signed off by Ruairi, and travelled to Donegal for his grandfather's funeral, believing that would be the end of the issue for the weekend. But standing at his grandfather's coffin that night, he was approached by a priest who said loudly, 'So you're the fecker who's helping Ruairi Quinn close all of my schools.' The strength of feeling on the issue across rural Ireland could not be underestimated.

Back in Leinster House the following week, government and opposition TDs frequently clashed. Independent TD Michael Healy-Rae labelled Ruairi Quinn a disgrace, while Fianna Fáil's Niall Collins claimed the coalition had an 'anti-rural' agenda. Both Ruairi and Minister of State Ciarán Cannon argued strongly that it was scare-mongering to sug-gest schools would close as a result of the budget changes. The only issue, they argued, was that teacher numbers in some small schools would not be 'as advantageous' as they had been.

While the impact of this budget measure on rural commu-nities would continue to be hotly debated over the following years, there were even greater fears about the content of a report that was due for imminent publication. In January 2011, the outgoing minister Mary Coughlan had reluctantly commissioned a Value for Money and Policy Review of Small Schools, commonly referred to as the VFM review. Such reviews are regularly carried out to assess whether public spending is achieving value for money, and achieving public-policy objectives. But no VFM review in education had ever attained the level of interest as that into small schools. The consultation period for the VFM review had attracted an unprecedented total of 1,065 submissions from interested organizations and from the general public. This was another indication of how important an issue the small school was to local communities.

The combination of the ongoing VFM review and the December 2011 budget measures helped to instil fear in many communities that their schools would go the way of local banks, garda stations and post offices. Anxieties were stoked further by largely unchallenged claims in local news-papers of wholesale closure of small schools. Ciarán Cannon, for instance, was elected in the constituency of East Galway, a county which had seventy-two schools with under fifty pupils, the greatest number of schools on that scale in the country, and it wasn't too difficult for the opposition to raise parents' concerns. Most people were well aware of Colm McCarthy's An Bord Snip Nua report which in 2009 had rec-ommended merging small schools to save money. It said that if the country's 659 primary schools with fewer than fifty pupils merged, this would save three hundred teaching jobs at a cost saving of €18 million a year. Further mergers of the 851 schools in the fifty-to-a-hundred-pupil category would save two hundred additional posts, it said.

Older people had memories of what had happened between 1966 and 1973, when around 1,100 one and two-teacher schools closed. The decline in some rural communities was blamed on these closures, but there were other factors, includ-ing emigration abroad and migration to the cities. The closures were not without controversy, and one in particular – Scoil

Dhún Chaoin in Kerry – came to represent the clash between faceless Dublin bureaucrats and embattled local communities fighting for survival. Scoil Dhún Chaoin on the Dingle peninsula attracted public support and some unlikely allies, such as Conor Cruise O'Brien, and was officially reopened in 1973, after a three-year battle. The policy of forced amalgamations slowed down after that. Fine Gael was concerned that campaigning anew on saving small schools would allow Fianna Fáil to become the Lazarus party beating the bushes to protect rural Ireland.

There may have been good political reasons for turning a blind eye to the issue, but there were urgent educational reasons for looking at the future of small schools, of which Ireland has a disproportionately high number relative to our population. The country has nearly 3,200 primary schools, of which 45 per cent have fewer than a hundred pupils. One in five has only one or two teachers. More than 70 per cent of our schools are so small that the principal is required to teach a class as well as looking after administration, meeting parents, fundraising and trying to improve the quality of teaching in the other classes. Some small schools are so close to each other that amalgamation would have little or no impact on the local community. Despite the nostalgic view of them, there is no evidence that they are educationally better than large schools. But neither are larger schools automatically better. It all depends on the quality of the teachers and, in particular, the principals.

Within the department, under the leadership of Kevin McCarthy, a quietly efficient assistant secretary general, officials had done thorough work preparing the VFM report, which everybody assumed would eventually be published. Ruairi and his team were given a copy of the report in confidence on 9 June 2012, in advance of a detailed briefing by officials ten days later. It was a lengthy document, packed full of data and detail about the impact that various options would have on schools in terms of reorganization and savings.

The very notion of saving money in this context – no more than on special needs – was provocative to some people, but this was a Value for Money report after all. It was part of the normal review processes undertaken by all departments on an annual basis on selected areas of expend-iture. The point was to take top-of-the-head calculations, emotion and politics out of it and just get to grips with the data and apply some standardized measures of how well the system was delivering. However, the fear – and of course it wasn't entirely groundless – was that any small school could be in line for closure or amalgamation. Politicians think in terms of political fallout and would encounter a lot of grief from local interests if schools in their constituency faced an uncertain future and possibly closure.

What struck me on reading the report was the relatively small savings that would follow from several hundred indi-vidual battles if all of the possibilities looked at in the VFM review were ever implemented in full. Even if the least drastic options, such as amalgamating one- and two-teacher schools within a certain radius of each other, were implemented, it would still have led to significant political fallout. It would consume a lot of time on the part of officials and a lot of political capital by the government.

From late 2012 and into 2013, Ruairi was impatient to get the report published and to begin to make decisions on implementing elements of the recommendations. But we warned him that, while it was good policy, it was politically fraught and it was Fine Gael's most sensitive educational issue. It was running in parallel with two other contentious issues he was pushing at the same time – the introduction of a capital-assets test for higher-education grants and the controversial new enrolment policy for schools. As advisers, we were considering taking bets on which, if any, of the three would get past the Cabinet.

In the run-up to the 2013 teacher conferences, Ruairi gave an interview to the *Sunday Business Post* in which he revealed that the report was likely to say the optimum minimum number of teachers in a school would be four – he had spoken to the Taoiseach, who appeared to be comfortable with this element of the recommendations coming into the public domain. At the INTO congress he said that small schools could not stand still or never have their staffing levels changed, nor could teachers be immune from budget cuts. Whatever about the budget changes already announced, he stressed that no decisions had been taken about the VFM review, which had been undertaken to ascertain the facts in order to inform future decisions. 'It does not mean that any policy decision has been taken at this point or that any particular outcome is sought,' he said.

He got a frosty reception. He was heckled during parts of his speech, and about twenty INTO members held up signs calling for small rural schools to be protected. INTO president Anne Fay claimed that, as a result of the weekend newspaper report, a thousand schools now feared for their existence.

Meanwhile, department officials were drafting a memo for the Cabinet summarizing the report and outlining how Ruairi proposed to implement some of the recommendations. After discussions with Ruairi and ourselves, the memo was tweaked and then circulated, along with the VFM review, on eCabinet, in June. Predictably, it provoked a strong negative reaction from Fine Gael ministers. I briefed Aine Kilroy, who had raised concerns on behalf of her minister, Simon Coveney.

But before it got to the Cabinet, Enda Kenny unexpectedly dropped into Ruairi's office on the Ministerial Corridor and told him it was going to the Cabinet's Social Policy Committee first, on 24 June, a week or so later. But that particular committee meeting was caught up with other matters, especially the more pressing issue of special-needs pupils, so the meeting did not get to it.

When the memo was not dealt with at the 24 June committee meeting, we continued to try to get it and the report discussed at the Cabinet. However, we were not successful. A few weeks later, Mark Kennelly and I had a bit of a barney over the memo, as well as one on changes to enrolment policy, being pulled from the Cabinet agenda by the Taoiseach.

'Ruairi's head will spin off over this,' I said.

'Don't shoot the messenger,' was his response.

Ruairi wanted to phone the Taoiseach immediately he heard what had happened, but Enda was tied up at meetings in Brussels and was unavailable. It wouldn't be the only time Enda was unavailable to discuss a policy idea while, at home, his advisers were blocking any progress on his behalf.

The small-schools issue did get discussed at the Cabinet Social Policy Committee on Monday, 22 July, a meeting which was well attended by Fine Gael ministers. Enda arrived a few minutes late, sat down quickly and leaned forward to chair the meeting briskly. The first item was Minister of State Alex White's presentation of a policy on restricting sponsorship of events by alcohol companies, which was kicked down the road. Several Fine Gael ministers then left and didn't hang around for the presentation on small schools by Department of Education and Skills official Tony Dalton.

Enda's response was blunt – he felt it was offering a gift to the opposition. He was obviously reflecting the views of his colleagues on the backbenches and in the Cabinet on a very contentious issue for the biggest party in government. He swivelled around to Phil Hogan to get his reaction. Hogan described it as 'a political minefield'. Ruairi obviously pressed the case for change and there was a fair bit of discussion. A number of questions were raised about school transport and the issue of 'bad' teachers in small schools, something the Taoiseach had also raised with me in Galway sixteen months earlier. Brendan Howlin referred to the potential savings from implementing the report, particularly if smaller schools were merged into larger ones. But I had the impression that, as a former primary-school principal himself, he knew at that stage the report was going nowhere, and he didn't push it too much. There was some vague talk about setting up a merger fund to encourage schools to amalgamate, but it petered out. The discussion really was about politics rather than education. It seems obvious that even publishing the report would set up a political explosion as far as Fine Gael was concerned.

Ruairi said he would still like to push for a Cabinet decision to publish the report and government decisions on it, but Enda suggested coming back to the Social Policy Committee in September.

While he was despondent over the failed attempts to get the VFM review and, separately, the assets tests for higher-education grants discussed at the Cabinet, Ruairi succeeded in bringing at least one of his three controversial memos up for discussion and decision at a subsequent Cabinet meeting – the one dealing with a new enrolment policy. Progress of a sort.

The small-schools issue rumbled on for the rest of the year and into 2014, with frequent calls from the opposition parties for the publication of the VFM review. Publishing it before the local and European elections in May 2014 would indeed be a gift to the opposition, so it was decided by the Taoiseach's and Tánaiste's people to hold off again.

While we accepted that logic, we sought clarification from Mark Kennelly that we were only postponing it until after the local elections, but that we could move on it after that. It was made very clear to us, however, that this report was unlikely to see the light of day during the lifetime of this government. There was a genuine fear on the Fine Gael side that even publishing the report and walking away from it would somehow provide Fianna Fáil with an opportunity to paint the whole government as pursuing an anti-rural agenda. That was despite the fact that the report had originally been commissioned by Fianna Fáil.

In the meantime, outside the pressure-cooker atmosphere of Government Buildings, there was unanticipated new thinking from two very unlikely sources. The viability of schools in some areas was now becoming a matter of increasing concern to both the Catholic Church and the INTO, and both made it very clear that they were interested in having a dialogue on the future of small schools.

In the Church's case, it was not surprising, as the diminishing number of priests was necessitating a rethink of its local structures and its deployment of personnel. As well as affecting the number of Masses that could be provided in rural communities, it also affected the Church's ability to manage large numbers of rural schools. A new general secretary, Fr Tom Deenihan, was appointed to the Catholic Primary Schools Management Association. It was initially expected that he would focus almost exclusively on issues relating to the Catholic ethos of their schools and on resisting the development of pluralism in them. However, he turned out to have an enormous interest in much more practical support for schools. He got on well with Ruairi, who felt he was pragmatic and open to discussions about small schools.

Similarly, the INTO, while publicly a strong defender of small schools, knew the issue had to be tackled. Motions passed at the 2014 congress called for a threshold of twenty-five pupils to be introduced, and that any school falling below that threshold should automatically trigger a study of demographics in the area to determine the future viability of the school. The union's new president, Sean McMahon, was the principal of a three-teacher school in west Clare and therefore particularly interested in finding ways to make small schools viable. On paper, Sean McMahon was apparently the polar opposite of Ruairi – a rural, naturally conservative individual – and everything we thought we knew about him prior to meeting him led us to believe that he and Ruairi would be unlikely to have a positive relationship. But on this we were very wrong. The two men quickly bonded, and met and spoke regularly over the next few months.

Between these contacts, and the clear desire on the part of both the Church and the unions to make progress on this issue, we began to move slowly towards agreeing some form of protocol to facilitate schools in considering amalgamating. The last year of the budget measure announced in December 2011 – increasing the pupil–teacher ratio – was being implemented in the autumn of 2014. McMahon was pushing for this to be paused, allowing schools a chance to consider whether amalgamation might be an option for them before their staffing was reduced any further. But we didn't believe that this was possible unless the individual schools gave concrete assurances that they were genuinely exploring amalgamation.

We came tantalizingly close to an agreement under which the last year of the budget measure would be paused for any school that confirmed in writing that its board of management had entered discussions about amalgamation with the board of management of another school. We had a meeting in Maynooth between officials and advisers and representatives of the union and the Catholic school managers at which we hoped to seal the deal. But, unfortunately, it became clear that some in the INTO were developing cold feet, feeling that we were asking too much of schools in a short period of time.

And so no announcement could be made about a protocol and we had to return to the Taoiseach's people and advise them that our hoped-for first step – one which would have benefited greatly from unity between the Church, the unions and the state – was no longer a viable option. We simply couldn't risk proceeding without the full support of the INTO – the political campaigns would have just started all over again. So the budget measure has now been fully implemented and the VFM review remains sitting on a shelf. It will remain there until the government grasps the nettle, publishes it and starts a conversation about developing sustainable schools in all of our communities.

21. Calling time

Nobody asked Ruairi about his intentions, but from late 2013 into early 2014 those of us around him assumed his time in office was drawing to a close. We just didn't know when the axe would fall. The speculation was already building. In late November, on the weekend of the Labour Party conference in Enfield, the *Indo* led with a story predicting that both Ruairi and Pat Rabbitte would go in the shake-up the following year – doing nothing for Rabbitte's mood around the conference centre. Andrew Lynch in the *Herald* followed it up with an opinion piece saying it was time for 'old war-horses' like Quinn and Rabbitte to be put out to grass. The belief among other advisers was that the *Indo* story had been planted by Eamon Gilmore's people. And some Labour people were upfront about what they wanted, with Senator John Whelan (not a hugely influential figure within the party, but one who got a fair amount of media attention) talking about 'grey old men' who were out of touch with the people.

All of this media chatter was damaging, as it bolstered opponents of Ruairi's reforms, who said to their colleagues, 'Hold on for a while, he'll be gone soon.' It was a view I was increasingly picking up from sources in the universities, the Catholic Church and particularly the second-level teacher unions, who were trying to get as much change from the junior-cycle reforms as they could before demanding more from his successor. He wasn't quite a dead man walking politically, but some of the education partners were already thinking about the situation post-Ruairi Quinn.

There was also speculation that he might be going to Europe if Phil Hogan didn't get the job. I travelled with Ruairi to Strasbourg in early December, and while he clearly loved the European stage and was well received by MEPs, he never really expected to get the commissioner's job when Máire Geoghegan-Quinn's term ended. Phil Hogan was always going to be the Taoiseach's choice.

All the talk about a forthcoming Cabinet shake-up was against the backdrop of opinion polls that continued to deliver bad news for the government. It was increasingly obvious that a sense of drift had descended after the exit from the bail-out in December 2013, and equally clear that tensions were building up between the parties.

In late January, I was sitting beside Phil Hogan's special adviser Sean McKeown at a Cabinet committee meeting in the Sycamore Room when the Taoiseach entered the room and came straight over to us. He had upset Labour ministers that morning by not notifying them in advance of his decision to apologize to Louise O'Keeffe, who had just won a case in the European Court of Human Rights over the state's responsibility for the sexual abuse she had suffered as a pupil in a primary school. While there was a certain nervousness about the financial implications of the ruling – the fear being that it might open the floodgates for a torrent of claims – everybody agreed that an apology was merited after the abuse Louise O'Keeffe had suffered. However, ministers, advisers and officials had not discussed the wording of the apology and Gilmore's people were annoyed that the apology was sprung on them without any forewarning. Not even Ruairi, whose department would have to deal with the

fallout, was alerted. The Taoiseach was clearly aware of the
upset and quipped, 'I see the cattle got loose again this morning!' Even a townie like me understood the allusion: loose
cattle upset the neighbours. In early 2014, there were a lot of
cattle astray in Government Buildings.

You could pick up the tension at adviser level. In April,
Pat Leahy got it bang on in the *Sunday Business Post* when he
wrote about the near-break-up of the coalition over water
charges. Labour understood that the Taoiseach was about to
have a roll call of ministers for their votes at the Cabinet,
which was unheard of in the coalition until then. The Tánaiste
had told the Taoiseach on two occasions that Labour was
not ready for a discussion on water charges, and that Labour
wanted the issue delayed until after the local elections.

Labour ministers were doubly angry when the political
correspondents were given details of the €240 annual water
charges, clearly from a Fine Gael source. Instructions were
issued to Labour advisers to prepare ideas for a draft election
manifesto by the end of the week, just in case of a snap general election. Despite all of the disagreements between the
two parties over budgets, abortion and other issues, this was
the one occasion when the future of the coalition was in
grave doubt.

Meanwhile, both parties were having their own internal
problems. As usual, the problems were related to individuals.
In the case of Fine Gael, these included Frank Flannery, the
party's arch-strategist. I knew Flannery from our days in
UCG, when it was obvious, even then, that he was going
places. His subsequent presidency of USI was the starting
point for a long career in public service and in Fine Gael. I
met him from time to time in Leinster House – to which he
had a pass, supplied by Fine Gael. This gave him access to

the Ministerial Corridor. Now he was in trouble over the pay levels of the Rehab chief executive, Angela Kerins, and others in Rehab, where he had been a director. Questions were also being raised about his lobbying activities, and he faced calls to appear before the Public Accounts Committee (PAC) to answer questions about his membership of the Rehab board, his consultancy work for the disability charity, and his pension arrangements.

When he was asked about the Flannery situation, Ruairi told *Morning Ireland* in March that he often bumped into Frank Flannery on the Ministerial Corridor, and he spoke about things, 'but not in a lobbying kind of way'. His comment ratcheted up the pressure on Flannery to quit Rehab and give up his Leinster House pass. He did so, as well as announcing that he was leaving Fine Gael.

He wasn't the only big Fine Gael beast to be felled. Alan Shatter, probably the hardest-working member of the Cabinet, ran into a succession of controversies – over the alleged bugging of the Garda Síochána Ombudsman Commission's office; over rows with rank and file members of the force; over a breach of data protection regarding TD Mick Wallace; and over the way he dealt with allegations by a garda whistleblower, Sergeant Maurice McCabe. Shatter finally resigned after a report by senior counsel Seán Guerin was critical of his approach to investigating the McCabe complaints. Typically, less than an hour before his dramatic resignation on 7 May, he was on his feet in the Dáil taking questions in his role as Minister for Defence, not giving the slightest hint of what was to come.

There were also tensions within the Labour Party. A number of events were organized in Carlow on 28 April, attended by Minister Brendan Howlin and the party's Euro candidate,

Phil Prendergast. It took place just as an *Independent* opinion poll put support of the party at an alarming 6 per cent of the electorate. Prendergast upstaged everybody that morning and helped prepare the way for subsequent events when she said on *Morning Ireland* that Eamon Gilmore should resign as party leader if he could not get the message across to the voters.

Instructions were issued for a 'boots-on-the-ground' turn-out of all Labour advisers and staffers to drop leaflets in the Dublin area to try to save Emer Costello's European seat, the only one Labour had any hope of retaining. Although not a member of the party, out of curiosity I went around Rathmines and quickly realized how tedious and tiring leaf-leting is, especially when there was so little hope of success. I would never have made a good foot soldier for any party. Having been Ruairi's office organizer for more than two decades, Denise Rogers was down in the dumps over their prospects. She had seen an increased number of notices in windows saying 'No election leaflets'.

Before the elections, there was a flurry of good-news announcements, made in the vain hope of staving off the inevitable electoral drubbing. Sinn Féin and Fianna Fáil were the winners. For Fine Gael, it was bad, but for Labour the election was a disaster, or 'shellacking', as Joan Burton called it. The only surprise was the scale of the defeat for Labour, but as Pat Rabbitte told Sean O'Rourke, 'If John the Baptist was leading Labour, we wouldn't have done any better.' From having three MEPs elected in the previous European Parlia-ment, the party suddenly had none, and its stock of councillors had been slashed to a third of where it had been in 2009.

The Gilmore Gale that had brought the party to its biggest

ever number of seats in the general election three years earlier had clearly blown out. A heave was getting underway on the morning of Monday, 26 May, with the submission of a no-confidence motion in his leadership by TDs Ciara Conway, Dominic Hannigan, Ged Nash, Derek Nolan, Aodhán Ó Ríordáin and Arthur Spring, and Senator John Gilroy. Word quickly circulated that they were being supported by junior minister Alex White. Labour ministers were called to a meeting with Gilmore in Iveagh House, and we all assumed this was the start of a defence of his leadership. But Gilmore abruptly announced that he was going.

'It was like somebody died,' was how a Labour Party press officer described the atmosphere on the Ministerial Corridor later that day. Dublin independent councillor Mannix Flynn said the Labour Party was behaving like the Americans fleeing Vietnam after the fall of Saigon.

Ruairi was furious over the heave and said on radio the next day that it was not Labour's way not to contact the leader about a planned vote of no confidence. Mark Garrett rang to thank us for our support but asked that there be no more comments please, as Gilmore wanted to go with dignity. Before the parliamentary party meeting the next day, Wednesday, Arthur Spring told me he wanted a quick word with Ruairi about the vote of no confidence from what was now being called the 'Goody-goody Gang' of eight. He wanted to apologize for the way it was done. Ged Nash was in touch with both Ruairi and Neil, anxious to ensure that his relationship with Ruairi had not been permanently damaged. Similar sentiments were expressed by other members of the gang at the Parliamentary Labour Party.

Alex White, who was clearly moving towards throwing his hat in the ring for leadership of the party, had an opportunity at that meeting to try to explain what had happened, and set out his stall for the leadership campaign. But he got carried away trying to explain that he hadn't really been the instigator of the heave – and Gilmore had to cut him off and tell him there was no need to continue rehashing the events of the week. He never did get to outline his pitch for leadership of the party and, in truth, his campaign was probably dead in the water at that point.

The PLP meeting was very emotional, from what I was later told. Gilmore gave a powerful speech, defending the decisions that the Labour Party had taken in government and expressing his pride in what the government had achieved. There was barely a dry eye as he paid tribute to his own team of advisers and personal staff for the service they had given him. Howlin made the perfect speech for a leadership candidate – setting out clearly what he believed Labour had accomplished, and the job of work that remained to be done during the lifetime of the government. But it would become clear over the next forty-eight hours that he wouldn't be a candidate – he realized he couldn't win. The other likely candidate was Joan Burton, but again an opportunity to start a campaign was missed – she spoke for so long that she ultimately had to be cut off by the PLP chairman, Jack Wall.

During that long meeting, there was a wide range of contributions – most of them thanking Gilmore for everything he had achieved, with many also pointing out where they believed improvements were needed. Aodhán Ó Ríordáin and Ciara Conway, both of whom had been involved in the heave, made emotional contributions in praise of Gilmore – both contributions seemed to jar with their actions of the previous days. Wicklow TD Anne Ferris lightened the mood momentarily by saying she had called Gilmore on Sunday night to ask if she would get a ministerial seat in a reshuffle.

The election for a successor to Gilmore was underway, with Joan Burton the obvious front runner, to be joined in battle a few days later by Alex White. Alan Kelly announced his intention to run for the deputy leadership of the party. Another candidate for the deputy's job was Sean Sherlock, the Cork East TD, whom we briefed a few days later for a Prime Time Special on higher education. If he hoped to use it as a pitch for election, he failed miserably – his performance was a study in the language of bureaucracy, and seemed devoid of political ideas. In a healthy sign for the party, two other candidates also emerged, Ciara Conway and Michael McCarthy. But it was to be a long-drawn-out business, with the results not known until Friday, 4 July.

In the meantime, Labour ministers pondered their futures. Ruairi knew he would not survive a reshuffle but was determined to get a lot of things finished before he left education. We developed a list of policy objectives that could be achieved during his final forty days in office and we updated this regularly with reports on where we were making progress or not. A glance at the list of press releases on the department's website from the end of May until the second week in July shows him living up to his Duracell-bunny image. He definitely wanted the report on inclusivity in primary schools published asap, which it was, as well as the establishment of the group to look at future funding of higher education. He set up a task force to help students in private language colleges that were closing. Among the department's publications were a new model for allocating resources for special-needs pupils, the first ever performance report into higher education and an implementation plan for the creation of twenty-first-century apprenticeships. He announced the details of what would be included in the Parents' and Students' Charter and got approval from the Cabinet for the drafting of the Technological Universities Bill.

'Save Ruairi Quinn and his Junior Cert reforms,' screamed a headline on the front page of the *Irish Daily Mail*, which carried a hugely complimentary piece inside by Matt Cooper lauding the minister and his plans. But we knew he wouldn't be in education to see them through. He might hope to see SOLAS realize some of its potential, to see more Catholic primary schools divested, and to see the new junior-cycle changes underway while he was still in politics as a backbencher. But it would be as an outsider, not as a minister.

Being a minister is probably the best job in Ireland. You're driven everywhere you go, you have advisers and a private secretary with you, officials when needed, you're sought out by the media, you get invitations to state banquets, embassy dinners, endless receptions, conferences at home and overseas where you meet international luminaries, and so on, and everywhere you go on an official visit you are always greeted by the top brass of the organization. People are constantly coming up to you at conferences or other events, telling you that you're doing a great job, that they have this wonderful idea, that they want to make a special case. Sometimes they have little to offer, but it's obvious that they just want to be in a minister's slipstream, all of which is flattering to the ego. It feeds into what Pat Carroll, Joan Burton's husband, once described to me as the 'psychic income' of being a minister. Over the decades, I've seen some TDs almost physically change when they get into Cabinet: they seem to grow in

stature, they straighten their shoulders, seek to acquire gravitas by speaking more slowly and with more emphasis. Take
that sense of power away from them and they can suffer
from withdrawal symptoms.

In January 2013, I ran into Seamus Cullimore, a former
Fianna Fáil TD from Wexford. Talking about life after the
Dáil, he said, 'Politics is like a drug. Once I got it out of my
system, I was OK.' He was a backbench TD, so what it's like
for a minister who is suddenly stripped of all the trappings
of office is hard to imagine. One former education minister
admitted privately to slipping into depression for over a year
after leaving office.

By the time he resigned, Ruairi Quinn was the Labour
Party's longest-ever-serving Cabinet minister, having served
in labour, public service, enterprise and employment, finance
and, finally, education and skills. The thoughtful and deliberate way he approached his exit from front-line politics made
it seem that somehow he might manage life after politics better than many of his predecessors. The manner and timing
of his announcement on the plinth outside Leinster House
was described as 'a master-class in dignity' by government
press secretary Feargal Purcell.

The six days between Ruairi's announcement on Wednesday, 2
July, and formally stepping down as minister the following
Tuesday, were surreal. Normally, ministers and advisers don't
get much notice if they are going. Boxes are left in their office
on the understanding that everything will be moved out
quickly to make way for the new inhabitants. But we had
plenty of time to pack, discard what we didn't want and take
home what we did. Rummaging through Ruairi's extensive
files, we found a signed copy of the Belfast Agreement,

which should really have been framed for its historical value. Ruairi's day books and diaries would also be of value to historians and researchers, given his tenure in different departments and particularly the key role he had played in many major EU decisions, including the creation of the euro.

His team had changed a little over his three years and four months in office and in these final days was made up of Neil, Deirdre Grant, myself, two relative newcomers, Jody Madigan, who had previously worked with Anne Ferris TD, and Niamh Hayes who returned to Leinster House to work with Ruairi as his parliamentary assistant after the reshuffle, when he became a backbench TD. The wisest of the team was Denise Rogers, Ruairi's hard-working office organizer for all of his political life. Denise was the one who asked the obvious question when we were discussing major educational changes – what does this mean for the ordinary parent or student? And there was one other 'honorary' team member, his sports-mad private secretary Ronnie Ryan, a civil servant who had worked with previous ministers. He was the go-to person when you wanted to talk to Ruairi urgently or pass on a crucial memo or piece of information.

After the harsh things he had said about officials when in opposition, Ruairi went on to forge a very good working relationship with them. Though occasionally he would complain that their sense of time was different from his – he was definitely a minister in a hurry. He had asked them to prove him wrong in his prejudices at his first Min-MAC meeting. They did that very quickly. Brigid McManus had retired in February 2012 and Ruairi had appointed Seán Ó Foghlú as her successor as secretary general. They got on well together, as they were both committed to educational reform.

Governments have a tendency to put in education ministers to calm things down in the run-up to an election, especially after a minister who had created 'noise in the system'. That week, I told Seán my money was on Jan O'Sullivan, a former teacher, to be his next minister. (And so it turned out. Her biggest challenge will be to get the junior-cycle reforms back on track after the unions' campaign to derail them.)

We were on the way out of the door, but the business of government continued to roll on, with endless emails about upcoming SOG (Senior Officials Group) meetings . . . memos on eCabinet . . . about a national sexual-health strategy . . . a national dementia strategy . . . a carers' strategy . . . It was like virtual ticker tape. Such are the vagaries of government business that on the very day he planned to announce his intention to quit, Ruairi was chosen to answer Dáil questions on education. He got Ciarán Cannon to take it on. He said he would be otherwise engaged.

22. Goodbye to all that

Ruairi regularly reminded us that we were really just temporary staff in the department. This was brought home to us first when we lost Ian O'Mara, who went off to use his fine legal brain in pursuit of the law, and then Nashie Grady, one of Ruairi's two drivers, announced that he was going to retire. Though Ruairi made it clear when he offered me the job that I would have it as long as he remained in office, when I accepted the offer of being Ruairi's special adviser I had intended to stay for just a year. One year turned into two and was now into its third. I told him I was thinking it was definitely time to go. My son's birthday party changed that.

It's really hard to organize a genuine surprise party, but my son's girlfriend, Karina Dolan, managed it for Conor's fortieth birthday. He assumed that they were just popping into Doheny & Nesbitt's to collect someone upstairs one evening at the end of August 2013. The expression 'his jaw dropped' accurately conveyed his reaction when he walked in to find dozens of waiting friends and family. And he was doubly surprised when a government minister came in with his birthday cake.

Later, over a glass or three of wine, Ruairi returned to the question of my proposed departure. I had told him I wanted to leave shortly, preferably before my daughter Maria married Al Healy at Ballybeg House in County Wicklow in October 2013. I wanted to have time to help them prepare for their big day. But Ruairi is nothing if not persistent and, as he had done previously, he managed to convince me to remain. For just a little longer.

I agreed to stay until the end of the year, which, of course, drifted into 2014 and continued until we all left in July. But the deal was that Neil Ward would take my job as full-time special adviser and I would do a three-day week, concentrating on a number of key policy areas, such as higher education, Church relations and the arts in education, while keeping an overview interest in other areas.

A three-day week never quite works out the way it's planned. When he heard what I was doing, the department's Alan Wall rang me to ask, 'John, can I arrange a meeting with you on the fourth day of your first three-day week?' Similarly, John Lynch, whom I had known for a long time from his days as director general of FÁS and as chair of CIÉ, phoned me up to tease me in his best hard chaw Dublin accent, saying, 'Walshe, I now regard you as a diminishing asset.'

However, the change would allow me to cut down on the endless meetings and cycle journeys to Government Buildings and play the odd game of golf. Just before Christmas 2013, I attended my final special advisers' session in the Sycamore Room. When the usual question was asked at the end of the meeting about forthcoming announcements, I said there were two from the Department of Education and Skills. The first was the imminent result of the latest ASTI ballot on reduced pay and allowances. If it went down, then schools would start to close in early January as the teachers would take industrial action. The second announcement was entirely unrelated to the first, I said, adding that by the time any school closures came I would be gone, which was greeted with laughter. I thanked them for their courtesy and cooperation since April 2011 and was delighted to receive words of praise from Colm O'Reardon and a round of applause from my now-former colleagues.

The changeover was due to take place early in 2014, but was delayed a bit because of a tweet by Neil which made the front page of the *Sunday World*. Some disgruntled DES staff member gave the newspaper a copy of one of his tweets on a Friday afternoon in which he joked that he had nothing to do, as he had cleared his inbox. The fact that he had filed everything away into folders and had cleared all outstanding queries attested to his efficiency, but he was portrayed as Do-nothing Adviser – overpaid, of course, as all advisers were usually described as being by the media and the opposition.

I described it as 'a storm in a tweet cup' and told him he had nothing to worry about. As expected, he fulfilled the role of full-time special adviser very well and went on to work with Jan O'Sullivan when she became minister. By that stage, he had learned the educational ropes. I had brought a know-ledge of the educational scene to the table and a contacts book of people we could work with or talk to in order to get a 'steer' on how the system would react to particular propos-als. By year three, Neil had developed his own contacts and knew whom we could do business with, and, more import-antly, who couldn't deliver on their organizational promises. His experience as a political adviser dealing with backbench-ers and ministers about individual school issues also helped, as did his membership of the Labour Party.

Not being a member of the party, I was sometimes at a disadvantage, particularly for deep background on rows involving the main party personalities, since I couldn't access the kind of institutional memory you build up when you're part of an organization for a long time. The Labour people had spent a long time in the political wilderness and fought and scrapped and made up and bonded together, so party members knew each other in a way I never could know them.

It didn't take me long, however, to work out that some Labour activists tended to drink in Toner's on Lower Baggot Street. It was beloved of a generation of them who had fallen somewhat out of favour during Pat Rabbitte's leadership of the party but who came in from the cold when Eamon Gilmore took over as leader. Those who thrived during the Rabbitte years tended to drink across the road in Doheny & Nesbitt's. I got to know and enjoy the company of both groups on the odd Friday-night visit to Baggot Street or after a late-evening meeting in nearby Government Buildings. The occasions were usually good fun, full of gossip and backbiting about colleagues in Labour and in Fine Gael. The opposition rarely got a mention, as they were not taken too seriously. Afterwards, my other son, Bryan, usually obliged me with a lift from the DART in Bray.

It was entirely appropriate that we ended up in Toner's the night Ruairi announced his resignation, drinking with some of the younger TDs, like Ged Nash and John Lyons, and the younger advisers and backroom staff in the party. Under new leadership, these were the people who would undertake the work necessary to persuade the electorate to return enough Labour TDs to make a significant impact in the next Dáil. If so, they would have to decide if they wished to form another coalition with Fine Gael, which Ruairi had always favoured.

But there would be fascinating times ahead in the Fine Gael–Labour relationship with Joan Burton as leader. I had seen Enda Kenny taking on board her views but also dismissing her in meetings. Indeed, I could recall one particularly revealing occasion when she began, characteristically, 'Taoiseach, I just want to say . . .', and he raised his palm to halt her and said, 'Joan, I'll come back to you later,' and turned to his left to Phil Hogan – 'Phil, what do you think?' That particular meeting ended, and she didn't get to speak again.

Since the leadership change, Burton's advisers, keen to draw a line between the old and the new regimes, refused to move into the third-floor offices previously occupied by Gilmore's people. Instead, they commandeered a suite of offices on the ground floor of Government Buildings. It will be interesting to see if the perceived 'upstairs downstairs' relationship takes on a more literal meaning as both parties begin to shape up for the next general election.

The new Colm O'Reardon is Burton's right-hand man, Ed Brophy. Brophy was described in Pat Leahy's *The Price of Power* as a 'whip-smart lawyer', which caused some mirth and the odd bit of jibing. Brophy had a trademark style – dark open-necked shirt and dark trousers. Over three years, I never saw him in a suit and tie, although I imagine he can suit up when required. His casual appearance belies his doggedness, and he can be formidably determined when he's supporting his boss. He and I had our run-ins during the establishment of SOLAS, but we never fell out.

Shortly after I started the job, Enda Kenny asked me what had most struck me since I had taken it on. I said it was the slow pace of change. Ministers have power but, as Ruairi often remarked, the caravan is only as fast as the slowest camel and, in education, that can be very slow indeed.

The other thing that struck me when I arrived in the job was how incredibly busy ministers are, at least in the bigger departments. Apart from endless meetings, all ministers get a huge volume of material to read in their own departments, never mind what's happening next door. I remember tackling one minister who wanted us to do something that contradicted a government decision the Cabinet had accepted. When I pointed that out to him, he responded, 'Ah sure, John, I don't have time to read everything.' At certain times of the year, such as just before the summer or Christmas breaks, that's very understandable. Assistant secretaries want to clear their desks of memos looking for a government decision or an agreement to publish an annual report before they go off on holidays. The result is that the Cabinet meetings immediately before the break are chock-a-block, with fifty or sixty items. When they come back from holidays, there might be as few as half a dozen items in the first Cabinet meeting after the break.

There should be a more efficient way of filtering memos and decisions for the Cabinet. The special advisers' meetings could also be more effective in advance of the Cabinet – discussing instead of ducking issues, as I saw too often. The Taoiseach's people were too protective at times, and effectively blocked items getting to the Cabinet, where they should be discussed, even if it meant a row.

And issues do come and go, burning hot one year and cool the next. In 2011 and 2012, fee-paying schools were the most urgent issue for Labour on the education front. In 2014, they rarely warranted a mention. Burning issues often reflect what the media are also highlighting, and they can also be fickle. In his first year of office, Ruairí was assailed in print on three front pages in the *Irish Independent* over a 'crisis' in maths teaching caused, the paper said, by not having a sufficient number of qualified maths teachers. The following year, the *Indo*, the *Times* and the *Examiner* all led with glowing reports about the improvement in maths results in the Leaving.

What also struck me was the fickleness of who's in and who's out, and for what reason. For a while in 2012, Ruairi was definitely 'out' as far as the Tánaiste's people were concerned. It may have been because the Tánaiste was very anxious to see a school in his constituency get a badly needed grant for refurbishment. Ruairi was clear – no queue-skipping. It would take its place in the queue. Clearly, the Tánaiste wasn't too happy. We decided to put on a charm offensive with Gilmore and his advisers to let them know the full extent of Ruairi's reform programme and how it could help Labour's standing in the polls. It worked, and we seemed to get back in good stead.

School buildings, of course, are one of those areas that every Minister for Education is pestered over by fellow party members. Politicians believe that providing more school buildings and improving the pupil–teacher ratio pays dividends at election time. It was one of the thoughts that crossed my mind as I was having a drink with Ruairi in the Members' Bar after last year's budget. Thanks to some nimble negotiations by our assistant secretary, Michael Keogh, and by Neil, in their dealings with DPER, it was the best budget we'd had. Ruairi got a fair number of congratulations for not actually making the pupil–teacher ratio worse than it already was. Essentially, he was being praised for not cutting spending rather than for doing what ministers instinctively really want to do, which is to increase spending. It made me wonder what political life was like in the old days, before austerity, when ministers handed out school buildings, new teaching posts, increased grants and other 'goodies' like sweets. Those were the days.

I enjoyed my time tramping the corridors of power, coming in as an observer from the outside to be an insider at the very heart of decision-making and government. I came into a new world – the world of Blueys (Fine Gaelers) and Trots (hard-left TDs), Shinners (Sinn Féin) and Binners (TDs Joe Higgins and Clare Daly); of Provowatch (keeping an eye on what Sinn Féin is doing by way of cuts in Northern Ireland while bemoaning similar ones in the Republic); of gaffes and cock-ups; of an alphabet soup of acronyms ... SOGs, MACs and Min-MACs; of inspiring vision and dispiriting cynicism; of damage limitation and announcements timed to get maximum political benefit; of a Taoiseach who is 'no Bambi' ... It was an administration that started in a state of shock, as it realized the money really was running out. When I left, it had steadied the ship of state but come unmoored itself.

The job was endlessly interesting and often exciting. What's not to love about a job that has you mixing with ministers and key decision-makers in education and the wider society? But the days were intense. I tried to keep office hours to a maximum of ten a day because, after numerous meetings, reading over a hundred demanding emails a day, writing and reading mountains of material, taking and making endless phone calls, and so on, I was spent and liable to start making mistakes. Some days there were so many calls and emails and so much material to read I felt like I was running hard to catch up with them all.

I agreed to chair a debate in Kevin Street DIT one morning, and when I switched on my phone two hours later found

I had missed eight phone calls, four texts, twenty-three emails and had four voice mails. Not surprisingly, I didn't do any more chairing or speaking at conferences. Lunch, launch and dinner invitations were routinely turned down because they took up too much time. Phone calls and emails were occasionally curt – but courteous, I hope, as they were dealt with under pressure of time.

Inevitably, some work spilled over into after hours. Unlike other ministers, Ruairi rarely rang at the weekend, and if he did he apologized, but I usually spent time on Sundays reading Cabinet papers on eCabinet in advance of Monday's special advisers' meetings. The work took its toll personally on friends and family, and I often wondered how special advisers with young families in other busy departments managed to find enough time for a decent home life.

I would miss many things – the excitement, the thrill of insider gossip, being part of something much bigger than I had imagined I ever would be, the sheer variety of issues to deal with on a daily basis and the friendships formed. I left with that inevitable sense of unfinished business you always have when you change job, and the inevitable question: what if we had done this or that in a different way?

But after over three years, the journey had ended. And there's only one way I can think of to measure the experience. Back in March 2011, when he offered me the job, Ruairi had called after me as I walked down Marlborough Street, 'And, John, we'll have fun!'

And we certainly did.

Acknowledgements

My thanks are due to Ruairi Quinn TD for my 'encore career' as his special adviser when he was Minister for Education and Skills. I am especially grateful to my partner, Mary, for putting up with the long hours I worked, and the even longer hours writing this book. I would particularly like to thank Patricia Deevy and Michael McLoughlin from Penguin Ireland for their encouragement and assistance with this publication.